The Scornful Lady by Francis Beaumont & John Fletcher

The English dramatists Francis Beaumont and John Fletcher, collaborated in their writing during the reign of James I of England (James VI of Scotland, 1567–1625; in England he reigned from 1603).

Beaumont & Fletcher began to collaborate as writers soon after they met. After notable failures of their solo works their first joint effort, Philaster, was a success and tragicomedy was the genre they explored and built upon. There would be many further successes to follow.

There is an account that at the time the two men shared everything. They lived together in a house on the Bankside in Southwark, "they also lived together in Bankside, sharing clothes and having one wench in the house between them." Or as another account puts it "sharing everything in the closest intimacy."

Whatever the truth of this they were now recognised as perhaps the best writing team of their generation, so much so, that their joint names was applied to all the works in which either, or both, had a pen including those with Philip Massinger, James Shirley and Nathan Field.

The first Beaumont and Fletcher folio of 1647 contained 35 plays; 53 plays were included in the second folio in 1679. Other works bring the total plays in the canon to about 55. However there appears here to have been some duplicity on the account of the publishers who seemed to attribute so many to the team. It is now thought that the work between solely by Beaumont and Fletcher amounts to approximately 15 plays, though of course further works by them were re-worked by others and the originals lost.

After Beaumont's early death in 1616 Fletcher continued to write and, at his height was, by many standards, the equal of Shakespeare in popularity until his own death in 1625.

Index of Contents

DRAMATIS PERSONAE

Elder Loveless, a Sutor to the Lady.
Young Loveless, a Prodigal.
Savil, Steward to Elder Loveless.
Lady and Martha, Two Sisters.
Younglove, or Abigal, a waiting Gentlewoman.
Welford, a Sutor to the Lady.
Sir Roger, Curate to the Lady.
Captain   }
Travailer   } Hangers on to Young Loveless.
Poet   }
Tabaco-man
Wenches.
Fidlers.
Morecraft, an Usurer.
A Rich Widow.
Attendants.

ACTUS PRIMUS

SCENA PRIMA

Enter the two **LOVELESSES**, **SAVIL** the Steward, and a **PAGE**.

ELDER LOVELESS
Brother, is your last hope past to mollifie Morecrafts heart about your Morgage?

YOUNG LOVELESS
Hopelesly past: I have presented the Usurer with a richer draught than ever Cleopatra swallowed; he hath suckt in ten thousand pounds worth of my Land, more than he paid for at a gulp, without Trumpets.

ELDER LOVELESS
I have as hard a task to perform in this house.

YOUNG LOVELESS
Faith mine was to make an Usurer honest, or to lose my Land.

ELDER LOVELESS
And mine is to perswade a passionate woman, or to leave the Land. Make the boat stay, I fear I shall begin my unfortunate journey this night, though the darkness of the night and the roughness of the waters might easily disswade an unwilling man.

SAVIL
Sir, your Fathers old friends hold it the sounder course for your body and estate to stay at home and marry, and propagate and govern in our Country, than to Travel and die without issue.

ELDER LOVELESS

Savil, you shall gain the opinion of a better servant, in seeking to execute, not alter my will, howsoever my intents succeed.

YOUNG LOVELESS

Yonder's Mistres Younglove, Brother, the grave rubber of your Mistresses toes.

[Enter **MISTRES YOUNGLOVE** the waiting woman.

ELDER LOVELESS

Mistres Younglove.

YOUNGLOVE

Master Loveless, truly we thought your sails had been hoist: my Mistres is perswaded you are Sea-sick ere this.

ELDER LOVELESS

Loves she her ill taken up resolution so dearly? Didst thou move her from me?

YOUNGLOVE

By this light that shines, there's no removing her, if she get a stiffe opinion by the end. I attempted her to day when they say a woman can deny nothing.

ELDER LOVELESS

What critical minute was that?

YOUNGLOVE

When her smock was over her ears: but she was no more pliant than if it hung about her heels.

ELDER LOVELESS

I prethee deliver my service, and say, I desire to see the dear cause of my banishment; and then for France.

YOUNGLOVE

I'le do't: hark hither, is that your Brother?

ELDER LOVELESS

Yes, have you lost your memory?

YOUNGLOVE

As I live he's a pretty fellow.

[Exit.

YOUNG LOVELESS

O this is a sweet Brache.

ELDER LOVELESS

Why she knows not you.

YOUNG LOVELESS
No, but she offered me once to know her: to this day she loves youth of Eighteen; she heard a tale how Cupid struck her in love with a great Lord in the Tilt-yard, but he never saw her; yet she in kindness would needs wear a Willow-garland at his Wedding. She lov'd all the Players in the last Queens time once over: she was struck when they acted Lovers, and forsook some when they plaid Murthers. She has nine Spur-royals, and the servants say she hoards old gold; and she her self pronounces angerly, that the Farmers eldest son, or her Mistres Husbands Clerk shall be, that Marries her, shall make her a joynture of fourscore pounds a year; she tells tales of the serving-men.

ELDER LOVELESS
Enough, I know her Brother. I shall intreat you only to salute my Mistres, and take leave, we'l part at the Stairs.

[Enter **LADY** and **WAITING WOMEN**.

LADY
Now Sir, this first part of your will is performed: what's the rest?

ELDER LOVELESS
First, let me beg your notice for this Gentleman my Brother.

LADY
I shall take it as a favour done to me, though the Gentleman hath received but an untimely grace from you, yet my charitable disposition would have been ready to have done him freer courtesies as a stranger, than upon those cold commendations.

YOUNG LOVELESS
Lady, my salutations crave acquaintance and leave at once.

LADY
Sir I hope you are the master of your own occasions.

[Exit **YOUNG LOVELESS** and **SAVIL**.

ELDER LOVELESS
Would I were so. Mistris, for me to praise over again that worth, which all the world, and you your self can see.

LADY
It's a cold room this, Servant.

ELDER LOVELESS
Mistris.

LADY
What think you if I have a Chimney for't, out here?

ELDER LOVELESS

Mistris, another in my place, that were not tyed to believe all your actions just, would apprehend himself wrong'd: But I whose vertues are constancy and obedience.

LADY

Younglove, make a good fire above to warm me after my servants Exordiums.

ELDER LOVELESS

I have heard and seen your affability to be such, that the servants you give wages to may speak.

LADY

'Tis true, 'tis true; but they speak to th' purpose.

ELDER LOVELESS

Mistris, your will leads my speeches from the purpose. But as a man—

LADY

A Simile servant? This room was built for honest meaners, that deliver themselves hastily and plainly, and are gone. Is this a time or place for Exordiums, and Similes and Metaphors? If you have ought to say, break into't: my answers shall very reasonably meet you.

ELDER LOVELESS

Mistris I came to see you.

LADY

That's happily dispatcht, the next.

ELDER LOVELESS

To take leave of you.

LADY

To be gone?

ELDER LOVELESS

Yes.

LADY

You need not have despair'd of that, nor have us'd so many circumstances to win me to give you leave to perform my command; is there a third?

ELDER LOVELESS

Yes, I had a third had you been apt to hear it.

LADY

I? Never apter. Fast, good servant, fast.

ELDER LOVELESS

'Twas to intreat you to hear reason.

LADY

Most willingly, have you brought one can speak it?

ELDER LOVELESS

Lastly, it is to kindle in that barren heart love and forgiveness.

LADY

You would stay at home?

ELDER LOVELESS

Yes Lady.

LADY

Why you may, and doubtlesly will, when you have debated that your commander is but your Mistris, a woman, a weak one, wildly overborn with passions: but the thing by her commanded, is to see Dovers dreadful cliffe, passing in a poor Water-house; the dangers of the merciless Channel 'twixt that and Callis, five long hours sail, with three poor weeks victuals.

ELDER LOVELESS

You wrong me.

LADY

Then to land dumb, unable to enquire for an English hoast, to remove from City to City, by most chargeable Post-horse, like one that rode in quest of his Mother tongue.

ELDER LOVELESS

You wrong me much.

LADY

And all these (almost invincible labours) performed for your Mistris, to be in danger to forsake her, and to put on new allegeance to some French Lady, who is content to change language with your laughter, and after your whole year spent in Tennis and broken speech, to stand to the hazard of being laught at, at your return, and have tales made on you by the Chamber-maids.

ELDER LOVELESS

You wrong me much.

LADY

Louder yet.

ELDER LOVELESS

You know your least word is of force to make me seek out dangers, move me not with toyes: but in this banishment, I must take leave to say, you are unjust: was one kiss forc't from you in publick by me so unpardonable? Why all the hours of day and night have seen us kiss.

LADY

'Tis true, and so you told the company that heard me chide.

ELDER LOVELESS
Your own eyes were not dearer to you than I.

LADY
And so you told 'em.

ELDER LOVELESS
I did, yet no sign of disgrace need to have stain'd your cheek: you your self knew your pure and simple heart to be most unspotted, and free from the least baseness.

LADY
I did: But if a Maids heart doth but once think that she is suspected, her own face will write her guilty.

ELDER LOVELESS
But where lay this disgrace? The world that knew us, knew our resolutions well: And could it be hop'd that I should give away my freedom; and venture a perpetual bondage with one I never kist? or could I in strict wisdom take too much love upon me, from her that chose me for her Husband?

LADY
Believe me; if my Wedding-smock were on,
Were the Gloves bought and given, the Licence come,
Were the Rosemary-branches dipt, and all
The Hipochrist and Cakes eat and drunk off,
Were these two armes incompast with the hands
Of Bachelors to lead me to the Church,
Were my feet in the door, were I John, said,
If John should boast a favour done by me,
I would not wed that year: And you I hope,
When you have spent this year commodiously,
In atchieving Languages, will at your return
Acknowledge me more coy of parting with mine eyes,
Than such a friend: More talk I hold not now
If you dare go.

ELDER LOVELESS
I dare, you know: First let me kiss.

LADY
Farewel sweet Servant, your task perform'd,
On a new ground as a beginning Sutor,
I shall be apt to hear you.

ELDER LOVELESS
Farewel cruel Mistres.

[Exit **LADY**.

[Enter **YOUNG LOVELESS** and **SAVIL**.

YOUNG LOVELESS
Brother you'l hazard the losing your tide to Gravesend: you have a long half mile by Land to Greenewich?

ELDER LOVELESS
I go: but Brother, what yet unheard of course to live, doth your imagination flatter you with? Your ordinary means are devour'd.

YOUNG LOVELESS
Course? why Horse-coursing I think. Consume no time in this: I have no Estate to be mended by meditation: he that busies himself about my fortunes may properly be said to busie himself about nothing.

ELDER LOVELESS
Yet some course you must take, which for my satisfaction resolve and open; if you will shape none, I must inform you that that man but perswades himself he means to live, that imagines not the means.

YOUNG LOVELESS
Why live upon others, as others have lived upon me.

ELDER LOVELESS
I apprehend not that: you have fed others, and consequently dispos'd of 'em: and the same measure must you expect from your maintainers, which will be too heavy an alteration for you to bear.

YOUNG LOVELESS
Why I'le purse; if that raise me not, I'le bet at Bowling-alleyes, or man Whores; I would fain live by others: but I'le live whilst I am unhang'd, and after the thought's taken.

ELDER LOVELESS
I see you are ty'd to no particular imploiment then?

YOUNG LOVELESS
Faith I may choose my course: they say nature brings forth none but she provides for them: I'le try her liberality.

ELDER LOVELESS
Well, to keep your feet out of base and dangerous paths, I have resolved you shall live as Master of my House. It shall be your care Savil to see him fed and cloathed, not according to his present Estate, but to his birth and former fortunes.

YOUNG LOVELESS
If it be refer'd to him, if I be not found in Carnation Jearsie-stockins, blew devils breeches, with the gards down, and my pocket i'th' sleeves, I'le n'er look you i'th' face again.

SAVIL

A comelier wear I wuss it is than those dangling slops.

ELDER LOVELESS
To keep you readie to do him all service peaceably, and him to command you reasonably, I leave these further directions in writing, which at your best leasure together open and read.

[Enter **YOUNGLOVE** to them with a Jewell.

ABIGAL
Sir, my Mistress commends her love to you in this token, and these words; it is a Jewell (she sayes) which as a favour from her she would request you to wear till your years travel be performed: which once expired, she will hastily expect your happy return.

ELDER LOVELESS
Return my service with such thanks, as she may imagine the heart of a suddenly over-joyed man would willingly utter, and you I hope I shall with slender arguments perswade to wear this Diamond, that when my Mistris shall through my long absence, and the approach of new Suitors, offer to forget me; you may cast your eye down to your finger, and remember and speak of me: She will hear thee better than those allied by birth to her; as we see many men much swayed by the Grooms of their Chambers, not that they have a greater part of their love or opinion on them, than on others, but for that they know their secrets.

ABIGAL
O' my credit I swear, I think 'twas made for me:
Fear no other Suitors.

ELDER LOVELESS
I shall not need to teach you how to discredit their beginning, you know how to take exception at their shirts at washing, or to make the maids swear they found plasters in their beds.

ABIGAL
I know, I know, and do not you fear the Suitors.

ELDER LOVELESS
Farewell, be mindfull, and be happie; the night calls me.

[Exeunt **OMNES** praeter **YOUNGLOVE**.

ABIGAL
The Gods of the Winds befriend you Sir; a constant and a liberal
Lover thou art, more such God send us.

[Enter **WELFORD**.

WELFORD
Let'em not stand still, we have rid.

ABIGAL

A suitor I know by his riding hard, I'le not be seen.

WELFORD
A prettie Hall this, no Servant in't? I would look freshly.

ABIGAL
You have delivered your errand to me then: there's no danger in a hansome young fellow: I'le shew my self.

WELFORD
Lady, may it please you to bestow upon a stranger the ordinary grace of salutation: Are you the Lady of this house?

ABIGAL
Sir, I am worthily proud to be a Servant of hers.

WELFORD
Lady, I should be as proud to be a Servant of yours, did not my so late acquaintance make me despair.

ABIGAL
Sir, it is not so hard to atchieve, but nature may bring it about.

WELFORD
For these comfortable words, I remain your glad Debtor. Is your Lady at home?

ABIGAL
She is no stragler Sir.

WELFORD
May her occasions admit me to speak with her?

ABIGAL
If you come in the way of a Suitor, No.

WELFORD
I know your affable vertue will be moved to perswade her, that a Gentleman benighted and strayed, offers to be bound to her for a nights lodging.

ABIGAL
I will commend this message to her; but if you aim at her body, you will be deluded: other women of the household of good carriage and government; upon any of which if you can cast your affection, they will perhaps be found as faithfull and not so coy.

[Exit **YOUNGLOVE.**

WELFORD

What a skin full of lust is this? I thought I had come a wooing, and I am the courted partie. This is right Court fashion: Men, Women, and all woo, catch that catch may. If this soft hearted woman have infused any of her tenderness into her Lady, there is hope she will be plyant. But who's here?

[Enter **SIR ROGER** the Curate.

SIR ROGER
Gad save you Sir. My Lady lets you know she desires to be acquainted with your name, before she confer with you?

WELFORD
Sir, my name calls me Welford.

SIR ROGER
Sir, you are a Gentleman of a good name. I'le try his wit.

WELFORD
I will uphold it as good as any of my Ancestors had this two hundred years Sir.

SIR ROGER
I knew a worshipfull and a Religious Gentleman of your name in the Bishoprick of Durham. Call you him Cousen?

WELFORD
I am only allyed to his vertues Sir.

SIR ROGER
It is modestly said: I should carry the badge of your Christianity with me too.

WELFORD
What's that, a Cross? there's a tester.

SIR ROGER
I mean the name which your God-fathers and God-mothers gave you at the Font.

WELFORD
'Tis Harry: but you cannot proceed orderly now in your Catechism: for you have told me who gave me that name. Shall I beg your name?

SIR ROGER
Roger.

WELFORD
What room fill you in this house?

SIR ROGER
More rooms than one.

WELFORD

The more the merrier: but may my boldness know, why your Lady hath sent you to decypher my name?

SIR ROGER

Her own words were these: To know whether you were a formerly denyed Suitor, disguised in this message: for I can assure you she delights not in Thalame: Hymen and she are at variance, I shall return with much hast.

[Exit **SIR ROGER**.

WELFORD

And much speed Sir, I hope: certainly I am arrived amongst a Nation of new found fools, on a Land where no Navigator has yet planted wit; if I had foreseen it, I would have laded my breeches with bells, knives, copper, and glasses, to trade with women for their virginities: yet I fear, I should have betrayed my self to a needless charge then: here's the walking night-cap again.

[Enter **SIR ROGER**.

SIR ROGER

Sir, my Ladies pleasure is to see you: who hath commanded me to acknowledge her sorrow, that you must take the pains to come up for so bad entertainment.

WELFORD

I shall obey your Lady that sent it, and acknowledge you that brought it to be your Arts Master.

SIR ROGER

I am but a Batchelor of Art, Sir; and I have the mending of all under this roof, from my Lady on her down-bed, to the maid in the Pease-straw.

WELFORD

A Cobler, Sir?

SIR ROGER

No Sir, I inculcate Divine Service within these Walls.

WELFORD

But the Inhabitants of this house do often imploy you on errands without any scruple of Conscience.

SIR ROGER

Yes, I do take the air many mornings on foot, three or four miles for eggs: but why move you that?

WELFORD

To know whether it might become your function to bid my man to neglect his horse a little to attend on me.

SIR ROGER

Most properly Sir.

WELFORD
I pray you doe so then: the whilst I will attend your lady
You direct all this house in the true way?

SIR ROGER
I doe Sir.

WELFORD
And this door I hope conducts to your Lady?

SIR ROGER
Your understanding is ingenious.

[Exeunt **SEVERALLY**.

[Enter **YOUNG LOVELESS** and **SAVIL**, with a writing.

SAVIL
By your favour Sir, you shall pardon me?

YOUNG LOVELESS
I shall bear your favour Sir, cross me no more; I say they shall come in.

SAVIL
Sir, you forget who I am?

YOUNG LOVELESS
Sir, I do not; thou art my Brothers Steward, his cast off mill-money, his Kitchen Arithmetick.

SAVIL
Sir, I hope you will not make so little of me?

YOUNG LOVELESS
I make thee not so little as thou art: for indeed there goes no more to the making of a Steward, but a fair Imprimis, and then a reasonable Item infus'd into him, and the thing is done.

SAVIL
Nay then you stir my duty, and I must tell you?

YOUNG LOVELESS
What wouldst thou tell me, how Hopps grow, or hold some rotten discourse of Sheep, or when our Lady-day falls? Prethee farewel, and entertain my friends, be drunk and burn thy Table-books: and my dear spark of velvet, thou and I.

SAVIL
Good Sir remember?

YOUNG LOVELESS

I do remember thee a foolish fellow, one that did put his trust in Almanacks, and Horse-fairs, and rose by Hony and Pot-butter.
Shall they come in yet?

SAVIL
Nay then I must unfold your Brothers pleasure, these be the lessons
Sir, he left behind him.

YOUNG LOVELESS
Prethee expound the first.

SAVIL
I leave to maintain my house three hundred pounds a year; and my
Brother to dispose of it.

YOUNG LOVELESS
Mark that my wicked Steward, and I dispose of it?

SAVIL
Whilest he bears himself like a Gentleman, and my credit falls not in him. Mark that my good young Sir, mark that.

YOUNG LOVELESS
Nay, if it be no more I shall fulfil it, whilst my Legs will carry me I'le bear my self Gentleman-like, but when I am drunk, let them bear me that can. Forward dear Steward.

SAVIL
Next it is my will, that he be furnished (as my Brother) with Attendance, Apparel, and the obedience of my people.

YOUNG LOVELESS
Steward this is as plain as your old Minikin-breeches. Your wisdom will relent now, will it not? Be mollified or—you understand me Sir, proceed?

SAVIL
Next, that my Steward keep his place, and power, and bound my
Brother's wildness with his care.

YOUNG LOVELESS
I'le hear no more of this Apocrypha, bind it by it self
Steward.

SAVIL
This is your Brothers will, and as I take it, he makes no mention of such company as you would draw unto you. Captains of Gallyfoists, such as in a clear day have seen Callis, fellows that have no more of God, than their Oaths come to: they wear swords to reach fire at a Play, and get there the oyl'd end of a Pipe, for their Guerdon: then the remnant of your Regiment, are wealthy Tobacco-Marchants, that set

up with one Ounce, and break for three: together with a Forlorn hope of Poets, and all these look like Carthusians, things without linnen: Are these fit company for my Masters Brother?

YOUNG LOVELESS
I will either convert thee (O thou Pagan Steward) or presently confound thee and thy reckonings, who's there? Call in the Gentlemen.

SAVIL
Good Sir.

YOUNG LOVELESS
Nay, you shall know both who I am, and where I am.

SAVIL
Are you my Masters Brother?

YOUNG LOVELESS
Are you the sage Master Steward, with a face like an old Ephemerides?

[Enter his **COMRADES, CAPTAIN, TRAVELLER,** &c.

SAVIL
Then God help us all I say.

YOUNG LOVELESS
I, and 'tis well said my old peer of France: welcome Gentlemen, welcome Gentlemen; mine own dear Lads y'are richly welcome. Know this old Harry Groat.

CAPTIN
Sir I will take your love.

SAVIL
Sir, you will take my Purse.

CAPTIN
And study to continue it.

SAVIL
I do believe you.

TRAVELLER
Your honorable friend and Masters Brother, hath given you to us for a worthy fellow, and so we hugg you Sir.

SAVIL
Has given himself into the hands of Varlets, not to be carv'd out.
Sir, are these the pieces?

YOUNG LOVELESS
They are the Morals of the Age, the vertues, men made of gold.

SAVIL
Of your gold you mean Sir.

YOUNG LOVELESS
This is a man of War, and cryes go on, and wears his colours.

SAVIL
In's nose.

YOUNG LOVELESS
In the fragrant field. This is a Traveller Sir, knows men and manners, and has plow'd up the Sea so far till both the Poles have knockt, has seen the Sun take Coach, and can distinguish the colour of his Horses, and their kinds, and had a Flanders-Mare leapt there.

SAVIL
'Tis much.

TRAVELLER
I have seen more Sir.

SAVIL
'Tis even enough o' Conscience; sit down, and rest you, you are at the end of the world already. Would you had as good a Living Sir, as this fellow could lie you out of, he has a notable gift in't.

YOUNG LOVELESS
This ministers the smoak, and this the Muses.

SAVIL
And you the Cloaths, and Meat, and Money, you have a goodly generation of 'em, pray let them multiply, your Brother's house is big enough, and to say truth, h'as too much Land, hang it durt.

YOUNG LOVELESS
Why now thou art a loving stinkard. Fire off thy Annotations and thy Rent-books, thou hast a weak brain Savil, and with the next long Bill thou wilt run mad. Gentlemen, you are once more welcome to three hundred pounds a year; we will be freely merry, shall we not?

CAPTIN
Merry as mirth and wine, my lovely Loveless.

POET
A serious look shall be a Jury to excommunicate any man from our company.

TRAVELLER
We will not talk wisely neither?

YOUNG LOVELESS
What think you Gentlemen by all this Revenue in Drink?

CAPTIN
I am all for Drink.

TRAVELLER
I am dry till it be so.

POET
He that will not cry Amen to this, let him live sober, seem wise, and dye o'th' Coram.

YOUNG LOVELESS
It shall be so, we'l have it all in Drink, let Meat and Lodging go, they are transitory, and shew men meerly mortal: then we'l have Wenches, every one his Wench, and every week a fresh one: we'l keep no powdered flesh: all these we have by warrant, under the title of things necessary. Here upon this place I ground it, The obedience of my people, and all necessaries: your opinions Gentlemen?

CAPTIN
'Tis plain and evident that he meant Wenches.

SAVIL
Good Sir let me expound it?

CAPTIN
Here be as sound men, as your self Sir.

POET
This do I hold to be the interpretation of it: In this word Necessary, is concluded all that be helps to Man; Woman was made the first, and therefore here the chiefest.

YOUNG LOVELESS
Believe me 'tis a learned one; and by these words,
The obedience of my people, you Steward being one, are bound to fetch us Wenches.

CAPTIN
He is, he is.

YOUNG LOVELESS
Steward, attend us for instructions.

SAVIL
But will you keep no house Sir?

YOUNG LOVELESS
Nothing but drink Sir, three hundred pounds in drink.

SAVIL
O miserable house, and miserable I that live to see it! Good Sir keep some meat.

YOUNG LOVELESS
Get us good Whores, and for your part, I'le board you in an Alehouse, you shall have Cheese and Onions.

SAVIL
What shall become of me, no Chimney smoking? Well Prodigal, your Brother will come home.

[Exit.

YOUNG LOVELESS
Come Lads, I'le warrant you for Wenches, three hundred pounds in drink.

[Exeunt **OMNES**.

ACTUS SECUNDUS

SCENA PRIMA

Enter **LADY**, her Sister **MARTHA**, **WELFORD**, **YOUNGLOVE**, and **OTHERS**.

LADY
Sir, now you see your bad lodging, I must bid you good night.

WELFORD
Lady if there be any want, 'tis in want of you.

LADY
A little sleep will ease that complement.
Once more good night.

WELFORD
Once more dear Lady, and then all sweet nights.

LADY
Dear Sir be short and sweet then.

WELFORD
Shall the morrow prove better to me, shall I hope my sute happier by this nights rest?

LADY
Is your sute so sickly that rest will help it? Pray ye let it rest then till I call for it. Sir as a stranger you have had all my welcome: but had I known your errand ere you came, your passage had been straiter. Sir, good night.

WELFORD

So fair, and cruel, dear unkind good night.

[Exit **LADY**.

Nay Sir, you shall stay with me, I'le press your zeal so far.

SIR ROGER

O Lord Sir.

WELFORD

Do you love Tobacco?

SIR ROGER

Surely I love it, but it loves not me; yet with your reverence I'le be bold.

WELFORD

Pray light it Sir. How do you like it?

SIR ROGER

I promise you it is notable stinging geer indeed. It is wet Sir, Lord how it brings down Rheum!

WELFORD

Handle it again Sir, you have a warm text of it.

SIR ROGER

Thanks ever promised for it. I promise you it is very powerful, and by a Trope, spiritual; for certainly it moves in sundry places.

WELFORD

I, it does so Sir, and me especially to ask Sir, why you wear a Night-cap.

SIR ROGER

Assuredly I will speak the truth unto you: you shall understand Sir, that my head is broken, and by whom; even by that visible beast the Butler.

WELFORD

The Butler? certainly he had all his drink about him when he did it. Strike one of your grave Cassock? The offence Sir?

SIR ROGER

Reproving him at Tra-trip Sir, for swearing; you have the total surely.

WELFORD

You told him when his rage was set a tilt, and so he crackt your Canons. I hope he has not hurt your gentle reading: But shall we see these Gentlewomen to night.

SIR ROGER

Have patience Sir until our fellow Nicholas be deceast, that is, asleep: for so the word is taken: to sleep to dye, to dye to sleep, a very figure Sir.

WELFORD
Cannot you cast another for the Gentlewomen?

SIR ROGER
Not till the man be in his bed, his grave: his grave, his bed: the very same again Sir. Our Comick Poet gives the reason sweetly; Plenus rimarum est, he is full of loope-holes, and will discover to our Patroness.

WELFORD
Your comment Sir has made me understand you.

[Enter **MARTHA,** the Ladies Sister, and **YOUNGLOVE**, to them with a Posset.

SIR ROGER
Sir be addrest, the graces do salute you with the full bowl of plenty. Is our old enemy entomb'd?

ABIGAL
He's safe.

SIR ROGER
And does he snore out supinely with the Poet?

MARTHA
No, he out-snores the Poet.

WELFORD
Gentlewoman, this courtesie shall bind a stranger to you, ever your servant.

MARTHA
Sir, my Sisters strictness makes not us forget you are a stranger and a Gentleman.

ABIGAL
In sooth Sir, were I chang'd into my Lady, a Gentleman so well indued with parts, should not be lost.

WELFORD
I thank you Gentlewoman, and rest bound to you. See how this foul familiar chewes the Cud: From thee, and three and fifty good Love deliver me.

MARTHA
Will you sit down Sir, and take a spoon?

WELFORD
I take it kindly, Lady.

MARTHA

It is our best banquet Sir.

SIR ROGER
Shall we give thanks?

WELFORD
I have to the Gentlewomen already Sir.

MARTHA
Good Sir Roger, keep that breath to cool your part o'th' Posset, you may chance have a scalding zeal else; and you will needs be doing, pray tell your twenty to your self. Would you could like this Sir?

WELFORD
I would your Sister would like me as well Lady.

MARTHA
Sure Sir, she would not eat you: but banish that imagination; she's only wedded to her self, lyes with her self, and loves her self; and for another Husband than herself, he may knock at the gate, but ne're come in: be wise Sir, she's a Woman, and a trouble, and has her many faults, the least of which is, she cannot love you.

ABIGAL
God pardon her, she'l do worse, would I were worthy his least grief, Mistris Martha.

WELFORD
Now I must over-hear her.

MARTHA
Faith would thou hadst them all with all my heart; I do not think they would make thee a day older.

ABIGAL
Sir, will you put in deeper, 'tis the sweeter.

MARTHA
Well said old sayings.

WELFORD
She looks like one indeed. Gentlewoman you keep your word, your sweet self has made the bottom sweeter.

ABIGAL
Sir, I begin a frolick, dare you change Sir?

WELFORD
My self for you, so please you. That smile has turn'd my stomach: this is right the old Embleme of the Moyle cropping of Thistles: Lord what a hunting head she carries, sure she has been ridden with a Martingale. Now love deliver me.

SIR ROGER

Do I dream, or do I wake? surely I know not: am I rub'd off? Is this the way of all my morning Prayers? Oh Roger, thou art but grass, and woman as a flower. Did I for this consume my quarters in Meditation, Vowes, and wooed her in Heroical Epistles? Did I expound the Owl, and undertook with labour and expence the recollection of those thousand Pieces, consum'd in Cellars, and Tabacco-shops of that our honour'd Englishman Ni. Br.? Have I done this, and am I done thus too? I will end with the wise man, and say; He that holds a Woman, has an Eel by the tail.

MARTHA

Sir 'tis so late, and our entertainment (meaning our Posset) by this is grown so cold, that 'twere an unmannerly part longer to hold you from your rest: let what the house has be at your command Sir.

WELFORD

Sweet rest be with you Lady; and to you what you desire too.

ABIGAL

It should be some such good thing like your self then.

[Exeunt.

WELFORD

Heaven keep me from that curse, and all my issue. Good night Antiquity.

SIR ROGER

Solamen Miseris socios habuisse Doloris: but I alone.

WELFORD

Learned Sir, will you bid my man come to me? and requesting a greater measure of your learning, good night, good Master Roger.

SIR ROGER

Good Sir, peace be with you.

[Exit **SIR ROGER**.

WELFORD

Adue dear Domine. Half a dozen such in a Kingdom would make a man forswear confession: for who that had but half his wits about him, would commit the Counsel of a serious sin to such a cruel Nightcap? Why how now shall we have an Antick?

[Enter **SERVANT**.

Whose head do you carry upon your shoulders, that you jole it so against the Post? Is't for your ease? Or have you seen the Celler? Where are my slippers Sir?

SERVANT

Here Sir.

WELFORD
Where Sir? have you got the pot Verdugo? have you seen the Horses Sir?

SERVANT
Yes Sir.

WELFORD
Have they any meat?

SERVANT
Faith Sir, they have a kind of wholesome Rushes, Hay I cannot call it.

WELFORD
And no Provender?

SERVANT
Sir, so I take it.

WELFORD
You are merry Sir, and why so?

SERVANT
Faith Sir, here are no Oats to be got, unless you'l have 'em in Porredge: the people are so mainly given to spoon-meat: yonder's a cast of Coach-mares of the Gentlewomans, the strangest Cattel.

WELFORD
Why?

SERVANT
Why, they are transparent Sir, you may see through them: and such a house!

WELFORD
Come Sir, the truth of your discovery.

SERVANT
Sir, they are in tribes like Jewes: the Kitchin and the Dayrie make one tribe, and have their faction and their fornication within themselves; the Buttery and the Landry are another, and there's no love lost; the chambers are intire, and what's done there, is somewhat higher than my knowledge: but this I am sure, between these copulations, a stranger is kept vertuous, that is, fasting. But of all this the drink Sir.

WELFORD
What of that Sir?

SERVANT
Faith Sir, I will handle it as the time and your patience will give me leave. This drink, or this cooling Julip, of which three spoonfuls kills the Calenture, a pint breeds the cold Palsie.

WELFORD

Sir, you bely the house.

SERVANT
I would I did Sir. But as I am a true man, if 'twere but one degree colder, nothing but an Asses hoof would hold it.

WELFORD
I am glad on't Sir, for if it had proved stronger, you had been tongue ti'd of these commendations. Light me the candle Sir, I'le hear no more

[Exeunt.

[Enter **YOUNG LOVELESS** and his **COMRADES**, with **WENCHES**, and two **FIDDLERS**.

YOUNG LOVELESS
Come my brave man of war, trace out thy darling,
And you my learned Council, sit and turn boyes,
Kiss till the Cow come home, kiss close, kiss close knaves.
My Modern Poet, thou shalt kiss in couplets.

[Enter with Wine.

Strike up you merry varlets, and leave your peeping,
This is no pay for Fidlers.

CAPTIN
O my dear boy, thy Hercules, thy Captain
Makes thee his Hylas, his delight, his solace.
Love thy brave man of war, and let thy bounty
Clap him in Shamois: Let there be deducted out of our main potation
Five Marks in hatchments to adorn this thigh,
Crampt with this rest of peace, and I will fight
Thy battels.

YOUNG LOVELESS
Thou shalt hav't boy, and fly in Feather,
Lead on a March you Michers.

[Enter **SAVIL**.

SAVIL
O my head, O my heart, what a noyse and change is here! would I had been cold i'th' mouth before this day, and ne're have liv'd to see this dissolution. He that lives within a mile of this place, had as good sleep in the perpetual noyse of an Iron Mill. There's a dead Sea of drink i'th' Seller, in which goodly vessels lye wrackt, and in the middle of this deluge appear the tops of flagons and black jacks, like Churches drown'd i'th' marshes.

YOUNG LOVELESS

What, art thou come? My sweet Sir Amias welcome to Troy.
Come thou shalt kiss my Helen, and court her in a dance.

SAVIL
Good Sir consider?

YOUNG LOVELESS
Shall we consider Gentlemen? How say you?

CAPTIN
Consider? that were a simple toy i'faith, consider? whose moral's that? The man that cryes consider is our foe: let my steel know him.

YOUNG LOVELESS
Stay thy dead doing hand, he must not die yet: prethee be calm my Hector.

CAPTIN
Peasant slave, thou groom compos'd of grudgings, live and thank this Gentleman, thou hadst seen Pluto else. The next consider kills thee.

TRAVELLER
Let him drink down his word again in a gallon of Sack.

POET
'Tis but a snuffe, make it two gallons, and let him doe it kneeling in repentance.

SAVIL
Nay rather kill me, there's but a lay-man lost. Good Captain doe your office.

YOUNG LOVELESS
Thou shalt drink Steward, drink and dance my Steward. Strike him a horn-pipe squeakers, take thy striver, and pace her till she stew.

SAVIL
Sure Sir, I cannot dance with your Gentlewomen, they are too light for me, pray break my head, and let me goe.

CAPTIN
He shall dance, he shall dance.

YOUNG LOVELESS
He shall dance, and drink, and be drunk and dance, and be drunk again, and shall see no meat in a year.

POET
And three quarters?

YOUNG LOVELESS
And three quarters be it.

CAPTIN
Who knocks there? let him in.

[Enter **ELDER LOVELESS** disguised.

SAVIL
Some to deliver me I hope.

ELDER LOVELESS
Gentlemen, God save you all, my business is to one Master Loveless?

CAPTIN
This is the Gentleman you mean; view him, and take his Inventorie, he's a right one.

ELDER LOVELESS
He promises no less Sir.

YOUNG LOVELESS
Sir, your business?

ELDER LOVELESS
Sir, I should let you know, yet I am loth, yet I am sworn to't, would some other tongue would speak it for me.

YOUNG LOVELESS
Out with it i' Gods name.

ELDER LOVELESS
All I desire Sir is, the patience and sufferance of a man, and good Sir be not mov'd more.

YOUNG LOVELESS
Then a pottle of sack will doe, here's my hand, prethee thy business?

ELDER LOVELESS
Good Sir excuse me, and whatsoever you hear, think must have been known unto you, and be your self discreet, and bear it nobly.

YOUNG LOVELESS
Prethee dispatch me.

ELDER LOVELESS
Your Brother's dead Sir.

YOUNG LOVELESS
Thou dost not mean dead drunk?

ELDER LOVELESS

No, no, dead and drown'd at sea Sir.

YOUNG LOVELESS
Art sure he's dead?

ELDER LOVELESS
Too sure Sir.

YOUNG LOVELESS
I but art thou very certainly sure of it?

ELDER LOVELESS
As sure Sir, as I tell it.

YOUNG LOVELESS
But art thou sure he came not up again?

ELDER LOVELESS
He may come up, but ne're to call you Brother.

YOUNG LOVELESS
But art sure he had water enough to drown him?

ELDER LOVELESS
Sure Sir, he wanted none.

YOUNG LOVELESS
I would not have him want, I lov'd him better; here I forgive thee: and i'faith be plain, how do I bear it?

ELDER LOVELESS
Very wisely Sir.

YOUNG LOVELESS
Fill him some wine. Thou dost not see me mov'd, these transitorie toyes ne're trouble me, he's in a better place, my friend I know't. Some fellows would have cryed now, and have curst thee, and faln out with their meat, and kept a pudder; but all this helps not, he was too good for us, and let God keep him: there's the right use on't friend. Off with thy drink, thou hast a spice of sorrow makes thee dry: fill him another. Savill, your Master's dead, and who am I now Savill? Nay, let's all bear it well, wipe Savill wipe, tears are but thrown away: we shall have wenches now, shall we not Savill?

SAVIL
Yes Sir.

YOUNG LOVELESS
And drink innumerable.

SAVIL
Yes forsooth.

YOUNG LOVELESS
And you'll strain curtsie and be drunk a little?

SAVIL
I would be glad, Sir, to doe my weak endeavour.

YOUNG LOVELESS
You may be brought in time to love a wench too.

SAVIL
In time the sturdie Oak Sir.

YOUNG LOVELESS
Some more wine for my friend there.

ELDER LOVELESS
I shall be drunk anon for my good news: but I have a loving
Brother, that's my comfort.

YOUNG LOVELESS
Here's to you Sir, this is the worst I wish you for your news: and if I had another elder Brother, and say it were his chance to feed Haddocks, I should be still the same you see me now, a poor contented Gentleman. More wine for my friend there, he's dry again.

ELDER LOVELESS
I shall be if I follow this beginning. Well my dear Brother, if I scape this drowning, 'tis your turn next to sink, you shall duck twice before I help you. Sir I cannot drink more; pray let me have your pardon.

YOUNG LOVELESS
O Lord Sir, 'tis your modestie: more wine, give him a bigger glass; hug him my Captain, thou shalt be my chief mourner.

CAPTIN
And this my pennon: Sir, a full carouse to you, and to my Lord of Land here.

ELDER LOVELESS
I feel a buzzing in my brains, pray God they bear this out, and I'le ne're trouble them so far again. Here's to you Sir.

YOUNG LOVELESS
To my dear Steward, down o' your knees you infidel, you Pagan; be drunk and penitent.

SAVIL
Forgive me Sir, and I'le be any thing.

YOUNG LOVELESS
Then be a Baud, I'le have thee a brave Baud.

ELDER LOVELESS

Sir, I must take my leave of you, my business is so urgent.

YOUNG LOVELESS

Let's have a bridling cast before you go. Fill's a new stoupe.

ELDER LOVELESS

I dare not Sir, by no means.

YOUNG LOVELESS

Have you any mind to a wench? I would fain gratifie you for
the pains you took Sir.

ELDER LOVELESS

As little as to the t'other.

YOUNG LOVELESS

If you find any stirring do but say so.

ELDER LOVELESS

Sir, you are too bounteous, when I feel that itching, you shall asswage it Sir, before another: this only
and Farewell Sir. Your Brother when the storm was most extream, told all about him, he left a will which
lies close behind a Chimney in the matted Chamber: and so as well Sir, as you have made me able, I take
my leave.

YOUNG LOVELESS

Let us imbrace him all: if you grow drie before you end your business, pray take a baite here, I have a
fresh hogshead for you.

SAVIL

You shall neither will nor chuse Sir. My Master is a wonderfull fine Gentleman, has a fine state, a very
fine state Sir, I am his Steward Sir, and his man.

ELDER LOVELESS

Would you were your own sir, as I left you. Well I must cast about, or all sinks.

SAVIL

Farewell Gentleman, Gentleman, Gentleman.

ELDER LOVELESS

What would you with me sir?

SAVIL

Farewell Gentleman.

ELDER LOVELESS

O sleep Sir, sleep.

[Exit **ELDER LOVELESS**.

YOUNG LOVELESS
Well boyes, you see what's faln, let's in and drink, and give thanks for it.

CAPTIN
Let's give thanks for it.

YOUNG LOVELESS
Drunk as I live.

SAVIL
Drunk as I live boyes.

YOUNG LOVELESS
Why, now thou art able to discharge thine office, and cast up a reckoning of some weight; I will be knighted, for my state will bear it, 'tis sixteen hundred boyes: off with your husks, I'le skin you all in Sattin.

CAPTIN
O sweet Loveless!

SAVIL
All in Sattin? O sweet Loveless!

YOUNG LOVELESS
March in my noble Compeeres: and this my Countess shall be led by two: and so proceed we to the Will.

[Exeunt.

[Enter **MORECRAFT** the Usurer, and **WIDOW**.

MORECRAFT
And Widow as I say be your own friend: your husband left you wealthy, I and wise, continue so sweet duck, continue so. Take heed of young smooth Varlets, younger Brothers: they are worms that will eat through your bags: they are very Lightning, that with a flash or two will melt your money, and never singe your purse-strings: they are Colts, wench Colts, heady and dangerous, till we take 'em up, and make 'em fit for Bonds: look upon me, I have had, and have yet matter of moment girle, matter of moment; you may meet with a worse back, I'le not commend it.

WIDOW
Nor I neither Sir.

MORECRAFT
Yet thus far by your favour Widow, 'tis tuffe.

WIDOW

And therefore not for my dyet, for I love a tender one.

MORECRAFT
Sweet Widow leave your frumps, and be edified: you know my state, I sell no Perspectives, Scarfs, Gloves, nor Hangers, nor put my trust in Shoe-ties; and where your Husband in an age was rising by burnt figs, dreg'd with meal and powdered sugar, saunders, and grains, wormeseed and rotten Raisins, and such vile Tobacco, that made the footmen mangie; I in a year have put up hundreds inclos'd, my Widow, those pleasant Meadows, by a forfeit morgage: for which the poor Knight takes a lone chamber, owes for his Ale, and dare not beat his Hostess: nay more—

WIDOW
Good Sir no more, what ere my Husband was, I know what I am, and if you marry me, you must bear it bravely off Sir.

MORECRAFT
Not with the head, sweet Widow.

WIDOW
No sweet Sir, but with your shoulders: I must have you dub'd, for under that I will not stoop a feather. My husband was a fellow lov'd to toyle, fed ill, made gain his exercise, and so grew costive, which for that I was his wife, I gave way to, and spun mine own smocks course, and sir, so little: but let that pass, time, that wears all things out, wore out this husband, who in penitence of such fruitless five years marriage, left me great with his wealth, which if you'le be a worthie gossip to, be knighted Sir.

[Enter **SAVIL**.

MORECRAFT
Now, Sir, from whom come you? whose man are you Sir?

SAVIL
Sir, I come from young Master Loveless.

MORECRAFT
Be silent Sir, I have no money, not a penny for you, he's sunk, your Master's sunk, a perisht man Sir.

SAVIL
Indeed his Brother's sunk sir, God be with him, a perisht man indeed, and drown'd at Sea.

MORECRAFT
How saidst thou, good my friend, his Brother drown'd?

SAVIL
Untimely sir, at Sea.

MORECRAFT
And thy young Master left sole Heir?

SAVIL

Yes Sir.

MORECRAFT
And he wants money?

SAVIL
Yes, and sent me to you, for he is now to be knighted.

MORECRAFT
Widow be wise, there's more Land coming, widow be very wise, and give thanks for me widow.

WIDOW
Be you very wise, and be knighted, and then give thanks for me Sir.

SAVIL
What sayes your worship to this mony?

MORECRAFT
I say he may have mony if he please.

SAVIL
A thousand Sir?

MORECRAFT
A thousand Sir, provided any wise Sir, his Land lye for the payment, otherwise—

[Enter **YOUNG LOVELESS** and **COMRADES** to them.

SAVIL
He's here himself Sir, and can better tell you.

MORECRAFT
My notable dear friend, and worthy Master Loveless, and now right worshipfull, all joy and welcom.

YOUNG LOVELESS
Thanks to my dear incloser Master Morecraft, prethee old Angel gold, salute my family, I'le do as much for yours; this, and your own desires, fair Gentlewoman.

WIDOW
And yours Sir, if you mean well; 'tis a hansome Gentleman.

YOUNG LOVELESS
Sirrah, my Brother's dead.

MORECRAFT
Dead?

YOUNG LOVELESS

Dead, and by this time soust for Ember Week.

MORECRAFT
Dead?

YOUNG LOVELESS
Drown'd, drown'd at sea man, by the next fresh Conger that comes we shall hear more.

MORECRAFT
Now by my faith of my body it moves me much.

YOUNG LOVELESS
What, wilt thou be an Ass, and weep for the dead? why I thought nothing but a general inundation would have mov'd thee, prethe be quiet, he hath left his land behind him.

MORECRAFT
O has he so?

YOUNG LOVELESS
Yes faith, I thank him for't, I have all boy, hast any ready mony?

MORECRAFT
Will you sell Sir?

YOUNG LOVELESS
No not out right good Gripe; marry, a morgage or such a slight securitie.

MORECRAFT
I have no mony, Sir, for Morgage; if you will sell, and all or none, I'le work a new Mine for you.

SAVIL
Good Sir look before you, he'l work you out of all else: if you sell all your Land, you have sold your Country, and then you must to Sea, to seek your Brother, and there lye pickled in a Powdering tub, and break your teeth with Biskets and hard Beef, that must have watering Sir: and where's your 300 pounds a year in drink then? If you'l tun up the Straights you may, for you have no calling for drink there, but with a Canon, nor no scoring but on your Ships sides, and then if you scape with life, and take a Faggot boat and a bottle of Usquebaugh, come home poor men, like a tipe of Thames-street stinking of Pitch and Poor-John. I cannot tell Sir, I would be loth to see it.

CAPTIN
Steward, you are an Ass, a meazel'd mungril, and were it not again the peace of my soveraign friend here, I would break your fore-casting Coxcomb, dog I would even with my staffe of Office there. Thy Pen and Inkhorn Noble boy, the God of gold here has fed thee well, take mony for thy durt: hark and believe, thou art cold of constitution, thy eat unhealthful, sell and be wise; we are three that will adorn thee, and live according to thine own heart child; mirth shall be only ours, and only ours shall be the black eyed beauties of the time. Mony makes men Eternal.

POET

Do what you will, 'tis the noblest course, then you may live without the charge of people, only we four will make a Family, I and an Age that will beget new Annals, in which I'le write thy life my son of pleasure, equal with Nero and Caligula.

YOUNG LOVELESS
What men were they Captain?

CAPTIN
Two roaring Boys of Rome, that made all split.

YOUNG LOVELESS
Come Sir, what dare you give?

SAVIL
You will not sell Sir?

YOUNG LOVELESS
Who told you so Sir?

SAVIL
Good Sir have a care.

YOUNG LOVELESS
Peace, or I'le tack your Tongue up to your Roof. What money? speak.

MORECRAFT
Six thousand pound Sir.

CAPTIN
Take it, h'as overbidden by the Sun: bind him to his bargain quickly.

YOUNG LOVELESS
Come strike me luck with earnest, and draw the writings.

MORECRAFT
There's a Gods peny for thee.

SAVIL
Sir for my old Masters sake let my Farm be excepted, if I become his Tenant I am undone, my Children beggers, and my Wife God knows what: consider me dear Sir.

MORECRAFT
I'le have all or none.

YOUNG LOVELESS
All in, all in: dispatch the writings.

[Exit with **COMRADE**.

WIDOW
Go, thou art a pretty forehanded fellow, would thou wert wiser.

SAVIL
Now do I sensibly begin to feel my self a Rascal; would I could teach a School, or beg, or lye well, I am utterly undone; now he that taught thee to deceive and cousen, take thee to his mercy; so be it.

[Exit **SAVIL**.

MORECRAFT
Come Widow come, never stand upon a Knight-hood, 'tis a meer paper honour, and not proof enough for a Serjeant. Come, Come, I'le make thee—

WIDOW
To answer in short, 'tis this Sir. No Knight no Widow, if you make me any thing, it must be a Lady, and so I take my leave.

MORECRAFT
Farewel sweet Widow, and think of it.

WIDOW
Sir, I do more than think of it, it makes me dream Sir.

[Exit **WIDOW**.

MORECRAFT
She's rich and sober, if this itch were from her: and say I be at the charge to pay the Footmen, and the Trumpets, I and the Horsemen too, and be a Knight, and she refuse me then; then am I hoist into the subsidy, and so by consequence should prove a Coxcomb: I'le have a care of that. Six thousand pound, and then the Land is mine, there's some refreshing yet.

[Exit.

ACTUS TERTIUS

SCENA PRIMA

Enter **ABIGAL** and drops her Glove.

ABIGAL
If he but follow me, as all my hopes tell me, he's man enough, up goes my rest, and I know I shall draw him.

[Enter **WELFORD**.

WELFORD

This is the strangest pampered piece of flesh towards fifty, that ever frailty copt withal, what a trim lennoy here she has put upon me; these women are a proud kind of Cattel, and love this whorson doing so directly, that they will not stick to make their very skins Bawdes to their flesh. Here's Dogskin and Storax sufficient to kill a Hawk: what to do with it, besides nailing it up amongst Irish heads of Teere, to shew the mightiness of her Palm, I know not: there she is. I must enter into Dialogue. Lady you have lost your Glove.

ABIGAL

Not Sir, if you have found it.

WELFORD

It was my meaning Lady to restore it.

ABIGAL

'Twill be uncivil in me to take back a favour, Fortune hath so well bestowed Sir, pray wear it for me.

WELFORD

I had rather wear a Bell. But hark you Mistres, what hidden vertue is there in this Glove, that you would have me wear it? Is't good against sore eyes, or will it charm the Toothach? Or these red tops; being steept in white wine soluble, wil't kill the Itch? Or has it so conceal'd a providence to keep my hand from Bonds? If it have none of these and prove no more but a bare Glove of half a Crown a pair, 'twill be but half a courtesie, I wear two alwayes, faith let's draw cuts, one will do me no pleasure.

ABIGAL

The tenderness of his years keeps him as yet in ignorance, he's a well moulded fellow, and I wonder his bloud should stir no higher; but 'tis his want of company: I must grow nearer to him.

[Enter **ELDER LOVELESS** disguised.

ELDER LOVELESS

God save you both.

ABIGAL

And pardon you Sir; this is somewhat rude, how came you hither?

ELDER LOVELESS

Why through the doors, they are open.

WELFORD

What are you? And what business have you here?

ELDER LOVELESS

More I believe than you have.

ABIGAL

Who would this fellow speak with? Art thou sober?

ELDER LOVELESS
Yes, I come not here to sleep.

WELFORD
Prethee what art thou?

ELDER LOVELESS
As much (gay man) as thou art, I am a Gentleman.

WELFORD
Art thou no more?

ELDER LOVELESS
Yes more than thou dar'st be; a Souldier.

ABIGAL
Thou dost not come to quarrel?

ELDER LOVELESS
No, not with women; I come to speak here with a Gentlewoman.

ABIGAL
Why, I am one.

ELDER LOVELESS
But not with one so gentle.

WELFORD
This is a fine fellow.

ELDER LOVELESS
Sir, I am not fine yet. I am but new come over, direct me with your ticket to your Taylor, and then I shall be fine Sir. Lady if there be a better of your Sex within this house, say I would see her.

ABIGAL
Why am not I good enough for you Sir?

ELDER LOVELESS
Your way you'l be too good, pray end my business. This is another Sutor, O frail Woman!

WELFORD
This fellow with his bluntness hopes to do more than the long sutes of a thousand could; though he be sowre he's quick, I must not trust him. Sir, this Lady is not to speak with you, she is more serious: you smell as if you were new calkt; go and be hansome, and then you may sit with her Servingmen.

ELDER LOVELESS
What are you Sir?

WELFORD
Guess by my outside.

ELDER LOVELESS
Then I take you Sir, for some new silken thing wean'd from the Country, that shall (when you come to keep good company) be beaten into better manners. Pray good proud Gentlewoman, help me to your Mistress.

ABIGAL
How many lives hast thou, that thou talk'st thus rudely?

ELDER LOVELESS
But one, one, I am neither Cat nor Woman.

WELFORD
And will that one life, Sir, maintain you ever in such bold
sawciness?

ELDER LOVELESS
Yes, amongst a Nation of such men as you are, and be no worse for wearing, shall I speak with this Lady?

ABIGAL
No by my troth shall you not.

ELDER LOVELESS
I must stay here then?

WELFORD
That you shall not neither.

ELDER LOVELESS
Good fine thing tell me why?

WELFORD
Good angry thing I'le tell you:
This is no place for such companions,
Such lousie Gentlemen shall find their business
Better i'th' Suburbs, there your strong pitch perfume,
Mingled with lees of Ale, shall reek in fashion:
This is no Thames-street, Sir.

ABIGAL
This Gentleman informs you truly:
Prethee be satisfied, and seek the Suburbs,
Good Captain, or what ever title else,
The Warlike Eele-boats have bestowed upon thee,
Go and reform thy self, prethee be sweeter,
And know my Lady speaks with no Swabbers.

ELDER LOVELESS
You cannot talk me out with your tradition
Of wit you pick from Plays, go to, I have found ye:
And for you, Sir, whose tender gentle blood
Runs in your Nose, and makes you snuff at all,
But three pil'd people, I do let you know,
He that begot your worships Sattin-sute,
Can make no men Sir: I will see this Lady,
And with the reverence of your silkenship,
In these old Ornaments.

WELFORD
You will not sure?

ELDER LOVELESS
Sure Sir I shall.

ABIGAL
You would be beaten out?

ELDER LOVELESS
Indeed I would not, or if I would be beaten,
Pray who shall beat me? this good Gentleman
Looks as if he were o'th' peace.

WELFORD
Sir you shall see that: will you get you out?

ELDER LOVELESS
Yes, that, that shall correct your boys tongue.
Dare you fight, I will stay here still.

[They draw.

ABIGAL
O their things are out, help, help for Gods sake,
Madam; Jesus they foin at one another.

[Enter **LADY**.

Madam, why, who is within there?

LADY
Who breeds this rudeness?

WELFORD
This uncivil fellow;

He saies he comes from Sea, where I believe,
H'as purg'd away his manners.

LADY
Why what of him?

WELFORD
Why he will rudely without once God bless you,
Press to your privacies, and no denial
Must stand betwixt your person and his business;
I let go his ill Language.

LADY
Sir, have you business with me?

ELDER LOVELESS
Madam some I have,
But not so serious to pawn my life for't:
If you keep this quarter, and maintain about you
Such Knights o'th' Sun as this is, to defie
Men of imployment to ye, you may live,
But in what fame?

LADY
Pray stay Sir, who has wrong'd you?

ELDER LOVELESS
Wrong me he cannot, though uncivilly
He flung his wild words at me: but to you
I think he did no honour, to deny
The hast I come withal, a passage to you,
Though I seem course.

LADY
Excuse me gentle Sir, 'twas from my knowledge,
And shall have no protection. And to you Sir,
You have shew'd more heat than wit, and from your self
Have borrowed power, I never gave you here,
To do these vile unmanly things: my house
Is no blind street to swagger in; and my favours
Not doting yet on your unknown deserts
So far, that I should make you Master of my business;
My credit yet stands fairer with the people
Than to be tried with swords; and they that come
To do me service, must not think to win me
With hazard of a murther; if your love
Consist in fury, carry it to the Camp:
And there in honour of some common Mistress,

Shorten your youth, I pray be better temper'd:
And give me leave a while Sir.

WELFORD
You must have it.

[Exit **WELFORD**.

LADY
Now Sir, your business?

ELDER LOVELESS
First, I thank you for schooling this young fellow,
Whom his own follies, which he's prone enough
Daily to fall into, if you but frown,
Shall level him a way to his repentance:
Next, I should rail at you, but you are a Woman,
And anger's lost upon you.

LADY
Why at me Sir?
I never did you wrong, for to my knowledge
This is the first sight of you.

ELDER LOVELESS
You have done that,
I must confess I have the least curse in
Because the least acquaintance: But there be
(If there be honour in the minds of men)
Thousands when they shall know what I deliver,
(As all good men must share in't) will to shame
Blast your black memory.

LADY
How is this good Sir?

ELDER LOVELESS
'Tis that, that if you have a soul will choak it:
Y'ave kill'd a Gentleman.

LADY
I kill'd a Gentleman!

ELDER LOVELESS
You and your cruelty have kill'd him Woman,
And such a man (let me be angry in't)
Whose least worth weighed above all womens vertues
That are; I spare you all to come too: guess him now?

LADY

I am so innocent I cannot Sir.

ELDER LOVELESS

Repent you mean, you are a perfect Woman,
And as the first was, made for mans undoing.

LADY

Sir, you have mist your way, I am not she.

ELDER LOVELESS

Would he had mist his way too, though he had
Wandered farther than Women are ill spoken of,
So he had mist this misery, you Lady.

LADY

How do you do, Sir?

ELDER LOVELESS

Well enough I hope.
While I can keep my self out from temptations.

LADY

Leap into this matter, whither would ye?

ELDER LOVELESS

You had a Servant that your peevishness
Injoined to Travel.

LADY

Such a one I have
Still, and shall be griev'd 'twere otherwise.

ELDER LOVELESS

Then have your asking, and be griev'd he's dead;
How you will answer for his worth, I know not,
But this I am sure, either he, or you, or both
Were stark mad, else he might have liv'd
To have given a stronger testimony to th' world
Of what he might have been. He was a man
I knew but in his evening, ten Suns after,
Forc'd by a Tyrant storm our beaten Bark
Bulg'd under us; in which sad parting blow,
He call'd upon his Saint, but not for life,
On you unhappy Woman, and whilest all
Sought to preserve their Souls, he desperately
Imbrac'd a Wave, crying to all that saw it,

If any live, go to my Fate that forc'd me
To this untimely end, and make her happy:
His name was Loveless: And I scap't the storm,
And now you have my business.

LADY
'Tis too much.
Would I had been that storm, he had not perisht.
If you'l rail now I will forgive you Sir.
Or if you'l call in more, if any more
Come from this ruine, I shall justly suffer
What they can say, I do confess my self
A guiltie cause in this. I would say more,
But grief is grown too great to be delivered.

ELDER LOVELESS
I like this well: these women are strange things.
'Tis somewhat of the latest now to weep,
You should have wept when he was going from you,
And chain'd him with those tears at home.

LADY
Would you had told me then so, these two arms had been his Sea.

ELDER LOVELESS
Trust me you move me much: but say he lived, these were forgotten things again.

LADY
I, say you so? Sure I should know that voice: this is knavery. I'le fit you for it. Were he living Sir, I would perswade you to be charitable, I, and confess we are not all so ill as your opinion holds us. O my friend, what penance shall I pull upon my fault, upon my most unworthy self for this?

ELDER LOVELESS
Leave to love others, 'twas some jealousie
That turn'd him desperate.

LADY
I'le be with you straight: are you wrung there?

ELDER LOVELESS
This works amain upon her.

LADY
I do confess there is a Gentleman
Has born me long good will.

ELDER LOVELESS
I do not like that.

LADY

And vow'd a thousand services to me; to me, regardless of him: But since Fate, that no power can withstand, has taken from me my first, and best love, and to weep away my youth is a mere folly, I will shew you what I determine sir: you shall know all: Call M. Welford there: That Gentleman I mean to make the model of my Fortunes, and in his chast imbraces keep alive the memory of my lost lovely Loveless: he is somewhat like him too.

ELDER LOVELESS

Then you can love.

LADY

Yes certainly Sir?
Though it please you to think me hard and cruel,
I hope I shall perswade you otherwise.

ELDER LOVELESS

I have made my self a fine fool.

[Enter **WELFORD**.

WELFORD

Would you have spoke with me Madam?

LADY

Yes M. Welford, and I ask your pardon before this Gentleman for being froward: this kiss, and henceforth more affection.

ELDER LOVELESS

So, 'tis better I were drown'd indeed.

WELFORD

This is a sudden passion, God hold it.
This fellow out of his fear sure has
Perswaded her. I'le give him a new suit on't.

LADY

A parting kiss, and good Sir, let me pray you
To wait me in the Gallerie.

WELFORD

I am in another world, Madam where you please.

[Exit **WELFORD**.

ELDER LOVELESS

I will to Sea, and 't shall goe hard but I'le be drown'd indeed.

LADY

Now Sir you see I am no such hard creature,
But time may win me.

ELDER LOVELESS

You have forgot your lost Love.

LADY

Alas Sir, what would you have me do? I cannot call him back again with sorrow; I'le love this man as
dearly, and beshrow me I'le keep him far enough from Sea, and 'twas told me, now I remember me, by
an old wise woman, that my first Love should be drown'd, and see 'tis come about.

ELDER LOVELESS

I would she had told you your second should be hang'd too, and let that come about: but this is very
strange.

LADY

Faith Sir, consider all, and then I know you'le be of my mind: if weeping would redeem him, I would
weep still.

ELDER LOVELESS

But say that I were Loveless,
And scap'd the storm, how would you answer this?

LADY

Why for that Gentleman I would leave all the world.

ELDER LOVELESS

This young thing too?

LADY

That young thing too,
Or any young thing else: why, I would lose my state.

ELDER LOVELESS

Why then he lives still, I am he, your Loveless.

LADY

Alas I knew it Sir, and for that purpose prepared this Pageant: get you to your task. And leave these
Players tricks, or I shall leave you, indeed I shall. Travel, or know me not.

ELDER LOVELESS

Will you then marry?

LADY

I will not promise, take your choice. Farewell.

ELDER LOVELESS

There is no other Purgatorie but a Woman.
I must doe something.

[Exit **ELDER LOVELESS**.

[Enter **WELFORD**.

WELFORD
Mistress I am bold.

LADY
You are indeed.

WELFORD
You so overjoyed me Lady.

LADY
Take heed you surfeit not, pray fast and welcom.

WELFORD
By this light you love me extreamly.

LADY
By this, and to morrows light, I care not for you.

WELFORD
Come, come, you cannot hide it.

LADY
Indeed I can, where you shall never find it.

WELFORD
I like this mirth well Lady.

LADY
You shall have more on't.

WELFORD
I must kiss you.

LADY
No Sir.

WELFORD
Indeed I must.

LADY

What must be, must be; I'le take my leave, you have your parting blow: I pray commend me to those few friends you have, that sent you hither, and tell them when you travel next, 'twere fit you brought less bravery with you, and more wit, you'le never get a wife else.

WELFORD
Are you in earnest?

LADY
Yes faith. Will you eat Sir, your horses will be readie straight, you shall have a napkin laid in the butterie for ye.

WELFORD
Do not you love me then?

LADY
Yes, for that face.

WELFORD
It is a good one Ladie.

LADY
Yes, if it were not warpt, the fire in time may mend it.

WELFORD
Me thinks yours is none of the best Ladie.

LADY
No by my troth Sir; yet o' my conscience,
You would make shift with it.

WELFORD
Come pray no more of this.

LADY
I will not: Fare you well. Ho, who's within there? bring out the Gentlemans horses, he's in haste; and set some cold meat on the Table.

WELFORD
I have too much of that I thank you Ladie: take your Chamber when you please, there goes a black one with you Ladie.

LADY
Farewell young man.

[Exit **LADY**.

WELFORD

You have made me one, Farewell: and may the curse of a great house fall upon thee, I mean the Butler. The devil and all his works are in these women, would all of my sex were of my mind, I would make 'em a new Lent, and a long one, that flesh might be in more reverence with them.

[Enter **ABIGAL** to him.

ABIGAL
I am sorry M. Welford.

WELFORD
So am I, that you are here.

ABIGAL
How does my Ladie use you?

WELFORD
As I would use you, scurvilie.

ABIGAL
I should have been more kind Sir.

WELFORD
I should have been undone then. Pray leave me, and look to your sweet-meats; hark, your Ladie calls.

ABIGAL
Sir, I shall borrow so much time without offence.

WELFORD
Y'are nothing but offence, for Gods love leave me.

ABIGAL
'Tis strange my Ladie should be such a tyrant?

WELFORD
To send you to me, 'Pray goe stitch, good doe, y'are more trouble to me than a Term.

ABIGAL
I do not know how my good will, if I said love I lied not, should any way deserve this?

WELFORD
A thousand waies, a thousand waies; sweet creature let me depart in peace.

ABIGAL
What Creature Sir? I hope I am a woman.

WELFORD
A hundred I think by your noise.

ABIGAL
Since you are angrie Sir, I am bold to tell you that I am a woman, and a rib.

WELFORD
Of a roasted horse.

ABIGAL
Conster me that?

WELFORD
A Dog can doe it better; Farwell Countess, and commend me to your Ladie, tell her she's proud, and scurvie, and so I commit you both to your tempter.

ABIGAL
Sweet Mr. Welford.

WELFORD
Avoid old Satanus: Go daub your ruines, your face looks fouler than a storm: the Foot-man stayes for you in the Lobby Lady.

ABIGAL
If you were a Gentleman, I should know it by your gentle conditions: are these fit words to give a Gentlewoman?

WELFORD
As fit as they were made for ye: Sirrah, my horses. Farwell old Adage, keep your nose warm, the Rheum will make it horn else—

[Exit **WELFORD**.

ABIGAL
The blessings of a Prodigal young heir be thy companions Welford, marry come up my Gentleman, are your gums grown so tender they cannot bite? A skittish Filly will be your fortune Welford, and fair enough for such a packsaddle. And I doubt not (if my aim hold) to see her made to amble to your hand.

[Exit **ABIGAL**.

[Enter **YOUNG LOVELESS**, and **COMRADES, MORECRAFT, WIDOW, SAVIL**, and the rest.

CAPTAIN
Save thy brave shoulder, my young puissant Knight, and may thy back Sword bite them to the bone that love thee not, thou art an errant man, go on. The circumcis'd shall fall by thee. Let Land and labour fill the man that tills, thy sword must be thy plough, and Jove it speed. Mecha shall sweat, and Mahomet shall fall, and thy dear name fill up his monument.

YOUNG LOVELESS
It shall Captain, I mean to be a Worthy.

CAPTAIN
One Worthy is too little, thou shalt be all.

MORECRAFT
Captain I shall deserve some of your love too.

CAPTAIN
Thou shalt have heart and hand too, noble Morecraft, if them wilt lend me mony. I am a man of Garrison, be rul'd, and open to me those infernal gates, whence none of thy evil Angels pass again, and I will stile thee noble, nay Don Diego. I'le woo thy Infanta for thee, and my Knight shall feast her with high meats, and make her apt.

MORECRAFT
Pardon me Captain, y'are beside my meaning.

YOUNG LOVELESS
No Mr. Morecraft, 'tis the Captains meaning I should prepare her for ye.

CAPTAIN
Or provok her. Speak my modern man, I say provoke her.

POET
Captain, I say so too, or stir her to it. So say the Criticks.

YOUNG LOVELESS
But howsoever you expound it sir, she's very welcom, and this shall serve for witness. And Widow, since y'are come so happily, you shall deliver up the keyes, and free possession of this house, whilst I stand by to ratifie.

WIDOW
I had rather give it back again believe me, 'Tis a miserie to say you had it. Take heed?

YOUNG LOVELESS
'Tis past that Widow, come, sit down, some wine there, there is a scurvie banquet if we had it. All this fair house is yours Sir Savil?

SAVIL
Yes Sir.

YOUNG LOVELESS
Are your keyes readie, I must ease your burden.

SAVIL
I am readie Sir to be undone, when you shall call me to't.

YOUNG LOVELESS
Come come, thou shalt live better.

SAVIL

I shall have less to doe, that's all, there's half a dozen of my friends i'th' fields sunning against a bank, with half a breech among 'em, I shall be with 'em shortly. The care and continuall vexation of being rich, eat up this rascall. What shall become of my poor familie, they are no sheep, and they must keep themselves.

YOUNG LOVELESS

Drink Master Morecraft, pray be merrie all:
Nay and you will not drink there's no societie,
Captain speak loud, and drink: widow, a word.

CAPTAIN

Expound her throughly Knight. Here God o' gold, here's to thy fair possessions; Be a Baron and a bold one: leave off your tickling of young heirs like Trouts, and let thy Chimnies smoke. Feed men of war, live and be honest, and be saved yet.

MORECRAFT

I thank you worthie Captain for your counsel. You keep your Chimnies smoking there, your nostrils, and when you can, you feed a man of War, this makes you not a Baron, but a bare one: and how or when you shall be saved, let the Clark o'th' companie (you have commanded) have a just care of.

POET

The man is much moved. Be not angrie Sir, but as the Poet sings, let your displeasure be a short furie, and goe out. You have spoke home, and bitterly, to me Sir. Captain take truce, the Miser is a tart and a wittie whorson—

CAPTAIN

Poet, you feign perdie, the wit of this man lies in his fingers ends, he must tell all; his tongue fills his mouth like a neats tongue, and only serves to lick his hungrie chaps after a purchase: his brains and brimstone are the devils diet to a fat usurers head: To her Knight, to her: clap her aboard, and stow her. Where's the brave Steward?

SAVIL

Here's your poor friend, and Savil Sir.

CAPTAIN

Away, th'art rich in ornaments of nature. First in thy face, thou hast a serious face, a betting, bargaining, and saving face, a rich face, pawn it to the Usurer; a face to kindle the compassion of the most ignorant and frozen Justice.

SAVIL

'Tis such I dare not shew it shortly sir.

CAPTAIN

Be blithe and bonny steward: Master Morecraft, Drink to this man of reckoning?

MORECRAFT

Here's e'ne to him.

SAVIL

The Devil guide it downward: would there were in't an acre of the great broom field he bought, to sweep your durtie Conscience, or to choak ye, 'tis all one to me, Usurer.

YOUNG LOVELESS

Consider what I told you, you are young, unapt for worldly business: Is it fit one of such tenderness, so delicate, so contrarie to things of care, should stir and break her better meditations, in the bare brokage of a brace of Angels? or a new Kirtel, though it be Satten? eat by the hope of surfeits, and lie down only in expectation of a morrow, that may undo some easie hearted fool, or reach a widows curses? Let out mony, whose use returns the principal? and get out of these troubles, a consuming heir: For such a one must follow necessarily, you shall die hated, if not old and miserable; and that possest wealth that you got with pining, live to see tumbled to anothers hands, that is no more a kin to you, than you to his couzenage.

WIDOW

Sir you speak well, would God that charity had first begun here.

YOUNG LOVELESS

'Tis yet time. Be merrie, me thinks you want wine there, there's more i'th' house. Captain, where rests the health?

CAPTAIN

It shall goe round boy.

YOUNG LOVELESS

Say you can suffer this, because the end points at much profit, can you so far bow below your blood, below your too much beautie, to be a partner of this fellowes bed, and lie with his diseases? if you can, I will not press you further: yet look upon him: there's nothing in that hide-bound Usurer, that man of mat, that all decai'd, but aches, for you to love, unless his perisht lungs, his drie cough, or his scurvie. This is truth, and so far I dare speak yet: he has yet past cure of Physick, spaw, or any diet, a primitive pox in his bones; and o' my Knowledge he has been ten times rowell'd: ye may love him; he had a bastard, his own toward issue, whipt, and then cropt for washing out the roses, in three farthings to make 'em pence.

WIDOW

I do not like these Morals.

YOUNG LOVELESS

You must not like him then.

[Enter **ELDER LOVELESS**.

ELDER LOVELESS

By your leave Gentlemen?

YOUNG LOVELESS

By my troth sir you are welcom, welcom faith: Lord what a stranger you are grown; pray know this Gentlewoman, and if you please these friends here: we are merry, you see the worst on't; your house has been kept warm Sir.

ELDER LOVELESS
I am glad to hear it Brother, pray God you are wise too.

YOUNG LOVELESS
Pray Mr. Morecraft know my elder Brother, and Captain do you complement. Savil I dare swear is glad at heart to see you; Lord, we heard Sir you were drown'd at Sea, and see how luckily things come about!

MORECRAFT
This mony must be paid again Sir.

YOUNG LOVELESS
No Sir, pray keep the Sale, 'twill make good Tailors measures;
I am well I thank you.

WIDOW
By my troth the Gentleman has stew'd him in his own Sawce, I shall love him for't.

SAVIL
I know not where I am, I am so glad: your worship is the welcom'st man alive; upon my knees I bid you welcome home: here has been such a hurry, such a din, such dismal Drinking, Swearing and Whoring, 'thas almost made me mad: we have all liv'd in a continual Turnbal-street; Sir, blest be Heaven, that sent you safe again, now shall I eat and go to bed again.

ELDER LOVELESS
Brother dismiss these people.

YOUNG LOVELESS
Captain be gone a while, meet me at my old Randevouse in the evening, take your small Poet with you. Mr. Morecraft you were best go prattle with your learned Counsel, I shall preserve your mony, I was couzen'd when time was, we are quit Sir.

WIDOW
Better and better still.

ELDER LOVELESS
What is this fellow, Brother?

YOUNG LOVELESS
The thirsty Usurer that supt my Land off.

ELDER LOVELESS
What does he tarry for?

YOUNG LOVELESS

Sir to be Landlord of your House and State: I was bold to make a little sale Sir.

MORECRAFT
Am I overreach'd? if there be Law I'le hamper ye.

ELDER LOVELESS
Prethee be gone, and rave at home, thou art so base a fool I cannot laugh at thee: Sirrah, this comes of couzening, home and spare, eat Reddish till you raise your sums again. If you stir far in this, I'le have you whipt, your ears nail'd for intelligencing o'the Pillory, and your goods forfeit: you are a stale couzener, leave my house: no more.

MORECRAFT
A pox upon your house. Come Widow, I shall yet hamper this young
Gamester.

WIDOW
Good twelve i'th' hundred keep your way, I am not for your diet, marry in your own Tribe Jew, and get a Broker.

YOUNG LOVELESS
'Tis well said Widow: will you jog on Sir?

MORECRAFT
Yes, I will go, but 'tis no matter whither:
But when I trust a wild Fool, and a Woman,
May I lend Gratis, and build Hospitals.

YOUNG LOVELESS
Nay good Sir, make all even, here's a Widow wants your good word for me, she's rich, and may renew me and my fortunes.

ELDER LOVELESS
I am glad you look before you. Gentlewoman, here is a poor distressed younger Brother.

WIDOW
You do him wrong Sir, he's a Knight.

ELDER LOVELESS
I ask you mercy: yet 'tis no matter, his Knighthood is no inheritance I take it: whatsoever he is, he is your Servant, or would be, Lady. Faith be not merciless, but make a man; he's young and handsome, though he be my Brother, and his observances may deserve your Love: he shall not fail for means.

WIDOW
Sir you speak like a worthy Brother: and so much I do credit your fair Language, that I shall love your Brother: and so love him, but I shall blush to say more.

ELDER LOVELESS

Stop her mouth. I hope you shall not live to know that hour when this shall be repented. Now Brother I should chide, but I'le give no distaste to your fair Mistress. I will instruct her in't and she shall do't: you have been wild and ignorant, pray mend it.

YOUNG LOVELESS
Sir, every day now Spring comes on.

ELDER LOVELESS
To you good Mr. Savil and your Office, thus much I have to say: Y'are from my Steward become, first your own Drunkard, then his Bawd: they say y'are excellent grown in both, and perfect: give me your keys Sir Savil.

SAVIL
Good Sir consider whom you left me to.

ELDER LOVELESS
I left you as a curb for, not to provoke my Brothers follies: where's the best drink, now? come, tell me Savil; where's the soundest Whores? Ye old he Goat, ye dried Ape, ye lame Stallion, must you be leading in my house your Whores, like Fairies dance their night rounds, without fear either of King or Constable, within my walls? Are all my Hangings safe; my Sheep unfold yet? I hope my Plate is currant, I ha' too much on't. What say you to 300 pounds in drink now?

SAVIL
Good Sir forgive me, and but hear me speak?

ELDER LOVELESS
Me thinks thou shouldst be drunk still, and not speak, 'tis the more pardonable.

SAVIL
I will Sir, if you will have it so.

ELDER LOVELESS
I thank ye: yes, e'ne pursue it Sir: do you hear? get a Whore soon for your recreation: go look out Captain Broken-breech your fellow, and Quarrel if you dare: I shall deliver these Keys to one shall have more honesty, though not so much fine wit Sir. You may walk and gather Cresses fit to cool your Liver; there's something for you to begin a Diet, you'l have the Pox else. Speed you well, Sir Savil: you may eat at my house to preserve life; but keep no Fornication in the Stables.

[Exit **OMNES**.

SAVIL
Now must I hang my self, my friends will look for't.
Eating and sleeping, I do despise you both now:
I will run mad first, and if that get not pitty,
I'le drown my self, to a most dismal ditty.

[Exit **SAVIL**.

ACTUS QUARTUS

SCENA PRIMA

Enter **ABIGAL** sola.

ABIGAL
Alas poor Gentlewoman, to what a misery hath Age brought thee: to what a scurvy Fortune! Thou that hast been a Companion for Noblemen, and at the worst of those times for Gentlemen: now like a broken Servingman, must beg for favour to those, that would have crawl'd like Pilgrims to my Chamber but for an Apparition of me. You that be coming on, make much of fifteen, and so till five and twenty: use your time with reverence, that your profits may arise: it will not tarry with you, Ecce signum: here was a face, but time that like a surfeit eats our youth, plague of his iron teeth, and draw 'em for't, has been a little bolder here than welcome: and now to say the truth, I am fit for no man. Old men i'th' house of fifty, call me Granum; and when they are drunk, e'ne then, when Jone and my Lady are all one, not one will do me reason. My little Levite hath forsaken me, his silver sound of Cittern quite abolisht, his doleful hymns under my Chamber window, digested into tedious learning: well fool, you leapt a Haddock when you left him: he's a clean man, and a good edifier, and twenty nobles is his state de claro, besides his pigs in posse. To this good Homilist I have been ever stubborn, which God forgive me for, and mend my manners: and Love, if ever thou hadst care of forty, of such a piece of lape ground, hear my prayer, and fire his zeal so far forth that my faults in this renued impression of my love may shew corrected to our gentle reader.

[Enter **ROGER**.

See how negligently he passes by me: with what an Equipage Canonical, as though he had broken the heart of Bellarmine, or added something to the singing Brethren. 'Tis scorn, I know it, and deserve it, Mr. Roger.

SIR ROGER
Fair Gentlewoman, my name is Roger.

ABIGAL
Then gentle Roger?

SIR ROGER
Ungentle Abigal.

ABIGAL
Why M'r Roger will you set your wit to a weak womans?

SIR ROGER
You are weak indeed: for so the Poet sings.

ABIGAL
I do confess my weakness, sweet Sir Roger.

SIR ROGER

Good my Ladies Gentlewoman, or my good Ladies Gentlewoman (this trope is lost to you now) leave your prating, you have a season of your first mother in ye: and surely had the Devil been in love, he had been abused too: go Dalilah, you make men fools, and wear Fig-breeches.

ABIGAL

Well, well, hard hearted man; dilate upon the weak infirmities of women: these are fit texts, but once there was a time, would I had never seen those eyes, those eyes, those orient eyes.

SIR ROGER

I they were pearls once with you.

ABIGAL

Saving your reverence Sir, so they are still.

SIR ROGER

Nay, nay, I do beseech you leave your cogging, what they are, they are, they serve me without Spectacles I thank 'em.

ABIGAL

O will you kill me?

SIR ROGER

I do not think I can,
Y'are like a Copy-hold with nine lives in't.

ABIGAL

You were wont to bear a Christian fear about you:
For your own worships sake.

SIR ROGER

I was a Christian fool then: Do you remember what a dance you led me? how I grew qualm'd in love, and was a dunce? could expound but once a quarter, and then was out too: and then out of the stinking stir you put me in, I prayed for my own issue. You do remember all this?

ABIGAL

O be as then you were!

SIR ROGER

I thank you for it, surely I will be wiser Abigal: and as the Ethnick Poet sings, I will not lose my oyl and labour too. Y'are for the worshipfull I take it Abigal.

ABIGAL

O take it so, and then I am for thee!

SIR ROGER

I like these tears well, and this humbling also, they are Symptomes of contrition. If I should fall into my fit again, would you not shake me into a quotidian Coxcombe? Would you not use me scurvily again, and give me possets with purging Confets in't? I tell thee Gentlewoman, thou hast been harder to me, than a long pedigree.

ABIGAL

O Curate cure me: I will love thee better, dearer, longer: I will do any thing, betray the secrets of the main house-hold to thy reformation. My Ladie shall look lovingly on thy learning, and when true time shall point thee for a Parson, I will convert thy egges to penny custards, and thy tith goose shall graze and multiply.

SIR ROGER

I am mollified, as well shall testifie this faithfull kiss, and have a great care Mistris Abigal how you depress the Spirit any more with your rebukes and mocks: for certainly the edge of such a follie cuts it self.

ABIGAL

O Sir, you have pierc'd me thorow. Here I vow a recantation to those malicious faults I ever did against you. Never more will I despise your learning, never more pin cards and cony tails upon your Cassock, never again reproach your reverend nightcap, and call it by the mangie name of murrin, never your reverend person more, and say, you look like one of Baals Priests in a hanging, never again when you say grace laugh at you, nor put you out at prayers: never cramp you more, nor when you ride, get Sope and Thistles for you. No my Roger, these faults shall be corrected and amended, as by the tenour of my tears appears.

SIR ROGER

Now cannot I hold if I should be hang'd, I must crie too. Come to thine own beloved, and do even what thou wilt with me sweet, sweet Abigal I am thine own for ever: here's my hand, when Roger proves a recreant, hang him i'th' Bel-ropes.

[Enter **LADY** and **MARTHA**.

LADY

Why how now Master Roger, no prayers down with you to night? Did you hear the bell ring? You are courting: your flock shall fat well for it.

SIR ROGER

I humbly ask your pardon: I'le clap up Prayers, but stay a little,
and be with you again.

[Exit **ROGER**.

[Enter **ELDER LOVELESS**.

LADY

How dare you, being so unworthie a fellow,
Presume to come to move me any more?

ELDER LOVELESS
Ha, ha, ha.

LADY
What ails the fellow?

ELDER LOVELESS
The fellow comes to laugh at you, I tell you Ladie I would not for your Land, be such a Coxcomb, such a whining Ass, as you decreed me for when I was last here.

LADY
I joy to hear you are wise, 'tis a rare Jewel
In an Elder Brother: pray be wiser yet.

ELDER LOVELESS
Me thinks I am very wise: I do not come a wooing. Indeed I'le move no more love to your Ladiship.

LADY
What makes you here then?

ELDER LOVELESS
Only to see you and be merry Ladie: that's all my business. Faith let's be very merry. Where's little Roger? he's a good fellow: an hour or two well spent in wholesome mirth, is worth a thousand of these puling passions. 'Tis an ill world for Lovers.

LADY
They were never fewer.

ELDER LOVELESS
I thank God there's one less for me Ladie.

LADY
You were never any Sir.

ELDER LOVELESS
Till now, and now I am the prettiest fellow.

LADY
You talk like a Tailor Sir.

ELDER LOVELESS
Me thinks your faces are no such fine things now.

LADY
Why did you tell me you were wise? Lord what a lying age is this, where will you mend these faces?

ELDER LOVELESS
A Hogs face soust is worth a hundred of 'em.

LADY

Sure you had a Sow to your Mother.

ELDER LOVELESS

She brought such fine white Pigs as you, fit for none but Parsons Ladie.

LADY

'Tis well you will allow us our Clergie yet.

ELDER LOVELESS

That shall not save you. O that I were in love again with a wish.

LADY

By this light you are a scurvie fellow, pray be gone.

ELDER LOVELESS

You know I am a clean skin'd man.

LADY

Do I know it?

ELDER LOVELESS

Come, come, you would know it; that's as good: but not a snap, never long for't, not a snap dear Ladie.

LADY

Hark ye Sir, hark ye, get ye to the Suburbs, there's horse flesh for such hounds: will you goe Sir?

ELDER LOVELESS

Lord how I lov'd this woman, how I worshipt this prettie calf with the white face here: as I live, you were the prettiest fool to play withall, the wittiest little varlet, it would talk: Lord how it talk't! and when I angred it, it would cry out, and scratch, and eat no meat, and it would say, goe hang.

LADY

It will say so still, if you anger it.

ELDER LOVELESS

And when I askt it, if it would be married, it sent me of an errand into France, and would abuse me, and be glad it did so.

LADY

Sir this is most unmanly, pray by gon.

ELDER LOVELESS

And swear (even when it twitter'd to be at me) I was unhansome.

LADY

Have you no manners in you?

ELDER LOVELESS
And say my back was melted, when God he knows, I kept it at a charge: Four Flaunders Mares would have been easier to me, and a Fencer.

LADY
You think all this is true now?

ELDER LOVELESS
Faith whether it be or no, 'tis too good for you. But so much for our mirth: Now have at you in earnest.

LADY
There is enough Sir, I desire no more.

ELDER LOVELESS
Yes faith, wee'l have a cast at your best parts now. And then the Devil take the worst.

LADY
Pray Sir no more, I am not so much affected with your commendations, 'tis almost dinner, I know they stay for you at the Ordinary.

ELDER LOVELESS
E'ne a short Grace, and then I am gone; You are a woman, and the proudest that ever lov'd a Coach: the scornfullest, scurviest, and most senceless woman; the greediest to be prais'd, and never mov'd though it be gross and open; the most envious, that at the poor fame of anothers face, would eat your own, and more than is your own, the paint belonging to it: of such a self opinion, that you think none can deserve your glove: and for your malice, you are so excellent, you might have been your Tempters tutor: nay, never cry.

LADY
Your own heart knows you wrong me: I cry for ye?

ELDER LOVELESS
You shall before I leave you.

LADY
Is all this spoke in earnest?

ELDER LOVELESS
Yes and more as soon as I can get it out.

LADY
Well out with't.

ELDER LOVELESS
You are, let me see.

LADY

One that has us'd you with too much respect.

ELDER LOVELESS
One that hath us'd me (since you will have it so) the basest, the most Foot-boy-like, without respect of
what I was, or what you might be by me; you have us'd me, as I would use a jade, ride him off's legs,
then turn him to the Commons; you have us'd me with discretion, and I thank ye. If you have many more
such pretty Servants, pray build an Hospital, and when they are old, pray keep 'em for shame.

LADY
I cannot think yet this is serious.

ELDER LOVELESS
Will you have more on't?

LADY
No faith, there's enough if it be true:
Too much by all my part; you are no Lover then?

ELDER LOVELESS
No, I had rather be a Carrier.

LADY
Why the Gods amend all.

ELDER LOVELESS
Neither do I think there can be such a fellow found i'th' world, to be in love with such a froward woman,
if there be such, they're mad, Jove comfort 'em. Now you have all, and I as new a man, as light, and
spirited, that I feel my self clean through another creature. O 'tis brave to be ones own man, I can see
you now as I would see a Picture, sit all day by you and never kiss your hand: hear you sing, and never
fall backward: but with as set a temper, as I would hear a Fidler, rise and thank you. I can now keep my
mony in my purse, that still was gadding out for Scarfes and Wastcoats: and keep my hand from Mercers
sheep-skins finely. I can eat mutton now, and feast my self with my two shillings, and can see a play for
eighteen pence again: I can my Ladie.

LADY
The carriage of this fellow vexes me. Sir, pray let me speak a little private with you, I must not suffer this.

ELDER LOVELESS
Ha, ha, ha, what would you with me?
You will not ravish me? Now, your set speech?

LADY
Thou perjur'd man.

ELDER LOVELESS
Ha, ha, ha, this is a fine exordium.
And why I pray you perjur'd?

LADY
Did you not swear a thousand thousand times you lov'd me best of all things?

ELDER LOVELESS
I do confess it: make your best of that.

LADY
Why do you say you do not then?

ELDER LOVELESS
Nay I'le swear it,
And give sufficient reason, your own usage.

LADY
Do you not love me then?

ELDER LOVELESS
No faith.

LADY
Did you ever think I lov'd you dearly?

ELDER LOVELESS
Yes, but I see but rotten fruits on't.

LADY
Do not denie your hand for I must kiss it, and take my last farewell, now let me die so you be happy.

ELDER LOVELESS
I am too foolish: Ladie speak dear Ladie.

LADY
No let me die.

[She swoons.

MARTHA
Oh my Sister!

ABIGAL
O my Ladie help, help.

MARTHA
Run for some Rosalis!

ELDER LOVELESS

I have plaid the fine ass: bend her bodie, Lady, best, dearest, worthiest Lady, hear your Servant, I am not as I shew'd: O wretched fool, to fling away the Jewel of thy life thus. Give her more air, see she begins to stir, sweet Mistress hear me!

LADY
Is my Servant well?

ELDER LOVELESS
In being yours I am so.

LADY
Then I care not.

ELDER LOVELESS
How do ye, reach a chair there; I confess my fault not pardonable, in pursuing thus upon such tenderness my wilfull error; but had I known it would have wrought thus with ye, thus strangely, not the world had won me to it, and let not (my best Ladie) any word spoke to my end disturb your quiet peace: for sooner shall you know a general ruine, than my faith broken. Do not doubt this Mistris, for by my life I cannot live without you. Come, come, you shall not grieve, rather be angrie, and heap infliction upon me: I will suffer. O I could curse my self, pray smile upon me. Upon my faith it was but a trick to trie you, knowing you lov'd me dearlie, and yet strangely that you would never shew it, though my means was all humilitie.

ALL
Ha, ha.

ELDER LOVELESS
How now?

LADY
I thank you fine fool for your most fine plot; this was a subtile one, a stiff device to have caught Dottrels with. Good senceless Sir, could you imagine I should swound for you, and know your self to be an arrant ass? I, a discovered one. 'Tis quit I thank you Sir. Ha, ha, ha.

MARTHA
Take heed Sir, she may chance to swound again.

ALL
Ha, ha, ha.

ABIGAL
Step to her Sir, see how she changes colour.

ELDER LOVELESS
I'le goe to hell first, and be better welcom.
I am fool'd, I do confess it, finely fool'd,
Ladie, fool'd Madam, and I thank you for it.

LADY
Faith 'tis not so much worth Sir:
But if I knew when you come next a burding,
I'le have a stronger noose to hold the Woodcock.

ALL
Ha, ha, ha.

ELDER LOVELESS
I am glad to see you merry, pray laugh on.

MARTHA
H'ad a hard heart that could not laugh at you Sir, ha, ha, ha.

LADY
Pray Sister do not laugh, you'le anger him,
And then hee'l rail like a rude Costermonger,
That School-boys had couzened of his Apples,
As loud and senceless.

ELDER LOVELESS
I will not rail.

MARTHA
Faith then let's hear him Sister.

ELDER LOVELESS
Yes, you shall hear me.

LADY
Shall we be the better by it then?

ELDER LOVELESS
No, he that makes a woman better by his words,
I'le have him Sainted: blows will not doe it.

LADY
By this light hee'll beat us.

ELDER LOVELESS
You do deserve it richly,
And may live to have a Beadle doe it.

LADY
Now he rails.

ELDER LOVELESS
Come scornfull Folly,

If this be railing, you shall hear me rail.

LADY
Pray put it in good words then.

ELDER LOVELESS
The worst are good enough for such a trifle,
Such a proud piece of Cobweblawn.

LADY
You bite Sir?

ELDER LOVELESS
I would till the bones crackt, and I had my will.

MARTHA
We had best muzzel him, he grows mad.

ELDER LOVELESS
I would 'twere lawfull in the next great sickness to have the Dogs spared, those harmless creatures, and knock i'th' head these hot continual plagues, women, that are more infectious. I hope the State will think on't.

LADY
Are you well Sir?

MARTHA
He looks as though he had a grievous fit o'th' Colick.

ELDER LOVELESS
Green-ginger will cure me.

ABIGAL
I'le heat a trencher for him.

ELDER LOVELESS
Durty December doe, Thou with a face as old as Erra Pater, such a Prognosticating nose: thou thing that ten years since has left to be a woman, outworn the expectation of a Baud; and thy dry bones can reach at nothing now, but gords or ninepins, pray goe fetch a trencher goe.

LADY
Let him alone, he's crack't.

ABIGAL
I'le see him hang'd first, is a beastly fellow to use a woman of my breeding thus; I marry is he: would I were a man, I'de make him eat his Knaves words!

ELDER LOVELESS

Tie your she Otter up, good Lady folly, she stinks worse than a Bear-baiting.

LADY
Why will you be angry now?

ELDER LOVELESS
Goe paint and purge, call in your kennel with you: you a Lady?

ABIGAL
Sirra, look to't against the quarter Sessions, if there be good behaviour in the world, I'le have thee bound to it.

ELDER LOVELESS
You must not seek it in your Ladies house then; pray send this Ferret home, and spin good Abigal. And Madam, that your Ladiship may know, in what base manner you have us'd my service, I do from this hour hate thee heartily; and though your folly should whip you to repentance, and waken you at length to see my wrongs, 'tis not the endeavour of your life shall win me; not all the friends you have, intercession, nor your submissive letters, though they spoke as many tears as words; not your knees grown to th' ground in penitence, nor all your state, to kiss you; nor my pardon, nor will to give you Christian burial, if you dye thus; so farewell. When I am married and made sure, I'le come and visit you again, and vex you Ladie. By all my hopes I'le be a torment to you, worse than a tedious winter. I know you will recant and sue to me, but save that labour: I'le rather love a fever and continual thirst, rather contract my youth to drink and sacerdote upon quarrels, or take a drawn whore from an Hospital, that time, diseases, and Mercury had eaten, than to be drawn to love you.

LADY
Ha, ha, ha, pray do, but take heed though.

ELDER LOVELESS
From thee, false dice, jades, Cowards, and plaguy Summers, good Lord deliver me.

[Exit **ELDER LOVELESS**.

LADY
But hark you Servant, hark ye: is he gon? call him again.

ABIGAL
Hang him Paddock.

LADY
Art thou here still? flie, flie, and call my Servant, flie or ne'r see me more.

ABIGAL
I had rather knit again than see that rascall, but I must doe it.

[Exit **ABIGAL**.

LADY

I would be loth to anger him too much; what fine foolery is this in a woman, to use those men most forwardly they love most? If I should lose him thus, I were rightly served. I hope he's not so much himself, to take it to th'heart: how now? will he come back?

[Enter **ABIGAL**.

ABIGAL
Never, he swears, whilst he can hear men say there's any woman living: he swore he would ha' me first.

LADY
Didst thou intreat him wench?

ABIGAL
As well as I could Madam. But this is still your way, to love being absent, and when he's with you, laugh at him and abuse him. There's another way if you could hit on't.

LADY
Thou saist true, get me paper, pen and ink, I'le write to him, I'de be loth he should sleep in's anger. Women are most fools when they think th'are wisest.

[Exit **OMNES**.

[Enter **YOUNG LOVELESS** and **WIDOW**, going to be Married, with them his **COMRADES**.

WIDOW
Pray Sir cast off these fellows, as unfitting for your bare knowledge, and far more your companie: is't fit such Ragamuffins as these are should bear the name of friends? and furnish out a civil house? ye're to be married now, and men that love you must expect a course far from your old carrier: if you will keep 'em, turn 'em to th' stable, and there make 'em grooms: and yet now consider it, such beggars once set o' horse back, you have heard will ride, how far you had best to look.

CAPTAIN
Hear you, you that must be Ladie, pray content your self and think upon your carriage soon at night, what dressing will best take your Knight, what wastcote, what cordial will do well i'th' morning for him, what triers have you?

WIDOW
What do you mean Sir?

CAPTAIN
Those that must switch him up: if he start well, fear not but cry Saint George, and bear him hard: when you perceive his wind growes hot and wanting, let him a little down, he's fleet, ne're doubt him, and stands sound.

WIDOW
Sir, you hear these fellows?

YOUNG LOVELESS

Merrie companions, wench, Merry companions.

WIDOW
To one another let 'em be companions, but good Sir not to you: you shall be civil and slip off these base trappings.

CAPTAIN
He shall not need, my most sweet Ladie Grocer, if he be civil, not your powdered Sugar, nor your Raisins shall perswade the Captain to live a Coxcomb with him; let him be civil and eat i'th' Arches, and see what will come on't.

POET
Let him be civil, doe: undo him; I, that's the next way. I will not take (if he be civil once) two hundred pound a year to live with him; be civil? there's a trim perswasion.

CAPTAIN
If thou beest civil Knight, as Jove defends it, get thee another nose, that will be pull'd off by the angry boyes for thy conversion: the children thou shalt get on this Civillian cannot inherit by the law, th'are Ethnicks, and all thy sport meer Moral leacherie: when they are grown, having but little in 'em, they may prove Haberdashers, or gross Grocers, like their dear Damm there: prethee be civil Knight, in time thou maist read to thy houshold, and be drunk once a year: this would shew finely.

YOUNG LOVELESS
I wonder sweet heart you will offer this, you do not understand these Gentlemen: I will be short and pithy: I had rather cast you off by the way of charge: these are Creatures, that nothing goes to the maintenance of but Corn and Water. I will keep these fellows just in the competencie of two Hens.

WIDOW
If you can cast it so Sir, you have my liking. If they eat less, I should not be offended: But how these Sir, can live upon so little as Corn and Water, I am unbelieving.

YOUNG LOVELESS
Why prethee sweet heart what's your Ale? is not that Corn and Water, my sweet Widow?

WIDOW
I but my sweet Knight where's the meat to this, and cloaths that they must look for?

YOUNG LOVELESS
In this short sentence Ale, is all included: Meat, Drink, and Cloth; These are no ravening Footmen, no fellows, that at Ordinaries dare eat their eighteen pence thrice out before they rise, and yet goe hungry to play, and crack more nuts than would suffice a dozen Squirrels; besides the din, which is damnable: I had rather rail, and be confin'd to a Boatmaker, than live amongst such rascals; these are people of such a clean discretion in their diet, of such a moderate sustenance, that they sweat if they but smell hot meat. Porredge is poison, they hate a Kitchin as they hate a Counter, and show 'em but a Feather-bed they swound. Ale is their eating and their drinking surely, which keeps their bodies clear, and soluble. Bread is a binder, and for that abolist even in their Ale, whose lost room fills an apple, which is more airy and of subtiler nature. The rest they take is little, and that little is little easie: For like strict men of order, they do correct their bodies with a bench, or a poor stubborn table; if a chimny offer it self with

some few broken rushes, they are in down: when they are sick, that's drunk, they may have fresh straw, else they do despise these worldly pamperings. For their poor apparel, 'tis worn out to the diet; new they seek none, and if a man should offer, they are angrie, scarce to be reconcil'd again with him: you shall not hear 'em ask one a cast doublet once in a year, which is modesty befitting my poor friends: you see their Wardrobe, though slender, competent: For shirts I take it, they are things worn out of their remembrance. Lousie they will be when they list, and mangie, which shows a fine variety: and then to cure 'em, a Tanners limepit, which is little charge, two dogs, and these; these two may be cur'd for 3. pence.

WIDOW
You have half perswaded me, pray use your pleasure: and my good friends since I do know your diet, I'le take an order, meat shall not offend you, you shall have Ale.

CAPTIN
We ask no more, let it be, mighty Lady: and if we perish, then our own sins on us.

YOUNG LOVELESS
Come forward Gentlemen, to Church my boys, when we have done, I'le give you cheer in bowles.

[Exeunt.

ACTUS QUINTUS

SCENA PRIMA

Enter **ELDER LOVELESS.**

ELDER LOVELESS
This senseless woman vexes me to th' heart, she will not from my memory: would she were a man for one two hours, that I might beat her. If I had been unhansome, old or jealous, 'thad been an even lay she might have scorn'd me; but to be young, and by this light I think as proper as the proudest; made as clean, as straight, and strong backt; means and manners equal with the best cloth of silver Sir i'th' kingdom: But these are things at some time of the Moon, below the cut of Canvas: sure she has some Meeching Rascal in her house, some Hind, that she hath seen bear (like another Milo) quarters of Malt upon his back, and sing with't, Thrash all day, and i'th' evening in his stockings, strike up a Hornpipe, and there stink two hours, and ne're a whit the worse man; these are they, these steel chin'd Rascals that undo us all. Would I had been a Carter, or a Coachman, I had done the deed e're this time.

[Enter **SERVANT**.

SERVANT
Sir, there's a Gentleman without would speak with you.

ELDER LOVELESS
Bid him come in.

[Enter **WELFORD**.

WELFORD
By your leave Sir.

ELDER LOVELESS
You are welcome, what's your will Sir?

WELFORD
Have you forgotten me?

ELDER LOVELESS
I do not much remember you.

WELFORD
You must Sir. I am that Gentleman you pleas'd to wrong, in your disguise, I have inquired you out.

ELDER LOVELESS
I was disguised indeed Sir if I wrong'd you, pray where and when?

WELFORD
In such a Ladies house, I need not name her.

ELDER LOVELESS
I do remember you, you seem'd to be a Sutor to that Lady?

WELFORD
If you remember this, do not forget how scurvily you us'd me: that was no place to quarrel in, pray you think of it; if you be honest you dare fight with me, without more urging, else I must provoke ye.

ELDER LOVELESS
Sir I dare fight, but never for a woman, I will not have her in my cause, she's mortal, and so is not my anger: if you have brought a nobler subject for our Swords, I am for you; in this I would be loth to prick my Finger. And where you say I wrong'd you, 'tis so far from my profession, that amongst my fears, to do wrong is the greatest: credit me we have been both abused, (not by our selves, for that I hold a spleen, no sin of malice, and may with man enough be best forgoten,) but by that willfull, scornful piece of hatred, that much forgetful Lady: for whose sake, if we should leave our reason, and run on upon our sense, like Rams, the little world of good men would laugh at us, and despise us, fixing upon our desperate memories the never-worn out names of Fools and Fencers. Sir 'tis not fear, but reason makes me tell you; in this I had rather help you Sir, than hurt you, and you shall find it, though you throw your self into as many dangers as she offers, though you redeem her lost name every day, and find her out new honours with your Sword, you shall but be her mirth as I have been.

WELFORD
I ask you mercy Sir, you have ta'ne my edge off: yet I would fain be even with this Lady.

ELDER LOVELESS

In which I'le be your helper: we are two, and they are two: two Sisters, rich alike, only the elder has the prouder Dowry: In troth I pity this disgrace in you, yet of mine own I am senceless: do but follow my Counsel, and I'le pawn my spirit, we'l overreach 'em yet; the means is this—

[Enter **SERVANT**.

SERVANT
Sir there's a Gentlewoman will needs speak with you, I cannot keep her out, she's entred Sir.

ELDER LOVELESS
It is the waiting woman, pray be not seen: sirrah hold her in discourse a while: hark in your ear, go and dispatch it quickly, when I come in, I'le tell you all the project.

WELFORD
I care not which I have.

[Exit **WELFORD**.

ELDER LOVELESS
Away, 'tis done, she must not see you: now Lady Guiniver what news with you?

[Enter **ABIGAL**.

ABIGAL
Pray leave these frumps Sir, and receive this letter.

ELDER LOVELESS
From whom good vanity?

ABIGAL
'Tis from my Lady Sir: Alas good soul, she cries and takes on!

ELDER LOVELESS
Do's she so good Soul? wou'd she not have a Cawdle? do's she send you with your fine Oratory goody Tully to tye me to believe again? bring out the Cat-hounds, I'le make you take a tree Whore, then with my tiller bring down your Gibship, and then have you cast, and hung up i'th' Warren.

ABIGAL
I am no beast Sir, would you knew it.

ELDER LOVELESS
Wou'd I did, for I am yet very doubtful; what will you say now?

ABIGAL
Nothing not I.

ELDER LOVELESS
Art thou a woman, and say nothing?

ABIGAL

Unless you'l hear me with more moderation, I can speak wise enough.

ELDER LOVELESS

And loud enough? will your Lady love me?

ABIGAL

It seems so by her letter, and her lamentations; but you are such another man.

ELDER LOVELESS

Not such another as I was, Mumps; nor will not be: I'le read her fine Epistle: ha, ha, ha, is not thy Mistress mad?

ABIGAL

For you she will be, 'tis a shame you should use a poor Gentlewoman so untowardly; she loves the ground you tread on; and you (hard heart) because she jested with you, mean to kill her; 'tis a fine conquest as they say.

ELDER LOVELESS

Hast thou so much moisture in the Whitleather hide yet, that thou canst cry? I wou'd have sworn thou hadst been touchwood five year since; nay let it rain, thy face chops for a shower like a dry Dunghil.

ABIGAL

I'le not indure this Ribauldry; farewel i'th' Devils name; if my Lady die, I'le be sworn before a Jury, thou art the cause on't.

ELDER LOVELESS

Do Maukin do, deliver to your Lady from me this: I mean to see her, if I have no other business: which before I'le want to come to her, I mean to go seek birds nests: yet I may come too: but if I come, from this door till I see her, will I think how to rail vildly at her; how to vex her, and make her cry so much, that the Physician if she fall sick upon't, shall find the cause to be want of Urine, and she remediless dye in her Heresie: Farewell old Adage, I hope to see the Boys make Potguns on thee.

ABIGAL

Th'art a vile man, God bless my issue from thee.

ELDER LOVELESS

Thou hast but one, and that's in thy left crupper, that makes thee hobble so; you must be ground i'th' breach like a Top, you'l ne're spin well else: Farewell Fytchock.

[Exeunt.

[Enter **LADY** alone.

LADY

Is it not strange that every womans will should track out new wayes to disturb her self? if I should call my reason to account, it cannot answer why I keep my self from mine own wish, and stop the man I love from his; and every hour repent again, yet still go on: I know 'tis like a man, that wants his natural sleep, and growing dull would gladly give the remnant of his life for two hours rest; yet through his frowardness, will rather choose to watch another man, drowsie as he, than take his own repose. All this I know: yet a strange peevishness and anger, not to have the power to do things unexpected, carries me away to mine own ruine: I had rather die sometimes than not disgrace in public him whom people think I love, and do't with oaths, and am in earnest then: O what are we! Men, you must answer this, that dare obey such things as we command. How now? what newes?

[Enter **ABIGAL**.

ABIGAL
Faith Madam none worth hearing.

LADY
Is he not come?

ABIGAL
No truly.

LADY
Nor has he writ?

ABIGAL
Neither. I pray God you have not undone your self.

LADY
Why, but what saies he?

ABIGAL
Faith he talks strangely.

LADY
How strangely?

ABIGAL
First at your Letter he laught extremely.

LADY
What, in contempt?

ABIGAL
He laught monstrous loud, as he would die, and when you wrote it I think you were in no such merry mood, to provoke him that way: and having done he cried Alas for her, and violently laught again.

LADY
Did he?

ABIGAL

Yes, till I was angry.

LADY
Angry, why? why wert thou angry? he did doe but well, I did deserve it, he had been a fool, an unfit man for any one to love, had he not laught thus at me: you were angry, that show'd your folly; I shall love him more for that, than all that ere he did before: but said he nothing else?

ABIGAL
Many uncertain things: he said though you had mockt him, because you were a woman, he could wish to do you so much favour as to see you: yet he said, he knew you rash, and was loth to offend you with the sight of one, whom now he was bound not to leave.

LADY
What one was that?

ABIGAL
I know not, but truly I do fear there is a making up there: for I heard the servants, as I past by some, whisper such a thing: and as I came back through the hall, there were two or three Clarks writing great conveyances in hast, which they said were for their Mistris joynture.

LADY
'Tis very like, and fit it should be so, for he does think, and reasonably think, that I should keep him with my idle tricks for ever ere he be married.

ABIGAL
At last he said, it should go hard but he would see you for your satisfaction.

LADY
All we that are called Women, know as well as men, it were a far more noble thing to grace where we are grace't, and give respect there where we are respected: yet we practise a wilder course, and never bend our eyes on men with pleasure, till they find the way to give us a neglect: then we, too late, perceive the loss of what we might have had, and dote to death.

[Enter **MARTHA**.

MARTHA
Sister, yonder's your Servant, with a Gentlewoman with him.

LADY
Where?

MARTHA
Close at the door.

LADY
Alas I am undone, I fear he is betroth'd,
What kind of woman is she?

MARTHA

A most ill favoured one, with her Masque on:
And how her face should mend the rest I know not.

LADY

But yet her mind was of a milder stuff than mine was.

[Enter **ELDER LOVELESS** and **WELFORD** in Womans apparel.

LADY

Now I see him, if my heart swell not again (away thou womans pride) so that I cannot speak a gentle word to him, let me not live.

ELDER LOVELESS

By your leave here.

LADY

How now, what new trick invites you hither?
Ha'you a fine device again?

ELDER LOVELESS

Faith this is the finest device I have now:
How dost thou sweet heart?

WELFORD

Why very well, so long as I may please
You my dear Lover. I nor can, nor will
Be ill when you are well, well when you are ill.

ELDER LOVELESS

O thy sweet temper! what would I have given, that Lady had been like thee: seest thou her? that face (my love) join'd with thy humble mind, had made a wench indeed.

WELFORD

Alas my love, what God hath done, I dare not think to mend. I use no paint, nor any drugs of Art, my hands and face will shew it.

LADY

Why what thing have you brought to shew us there? do you take mony for it?

ELDER LOVELESS

A Godlike thing, not to be bought for mony: 'tis my Mistris: in whom there is no passion, nor no scorn: what I will is for law; pray you salute her.

LADY

Salute her? by this good light, I would not kiss her for half my wealth.

ELDER LOVELESS

Why? why pray you?
You shall see me do't afore you; look you.

LADY
Now fie upon thee, a beast would not have don't.
I would not kiss thee of a month to gain a Kingdom.

ELDER LOVELESS
Marry you shall not be troubled.

LADY
Why was there ever such a Meg as this?
Sure thou art mad.

ELDER LOVELESS
I was mad once, when I lov'd pictures; for what are shape and colours else, but pictures? in that tawnie hide there lies an endless mass of vertues, when all your red and white ones want it.

LADY
And this is she you are to marry, is't not?

ELDER LOVELESS
Yes indeed is't.

LADY
God give you joy.

ELDER LOVELESS
Amen.

WELFORD
I thank you, as unknown for your good wish.
The like to you when ever you shall wed.

ELDER LOVELESS
O gentle Spirit!

LADY
You thank me? I pray
Keep your breath nearer you, I do not like it.

WELFORD
I would not willingly offend at all,
Much less a Lady of your worthie parts.

ELDER LOVELESS
Sweet, Sweet!

LADY
I do not think this woman can by nature be thus,
Thus ugly; sure she's some common Strumpet,
Deform'd with exercise of sin?

WELFORD
O Sir believe not this, for Heaven so comfort me as I am free from foul pollution with any man; my honour ta'ne away, I am no woman.

ELDER LOVELESS
Arise my dearest Soul; I do not credit it. Alas, I fear her tender heart will break with this reproach; fie that you know no more civility to a weak Virgin. 'Tis no matter Sweet, let her say what she will, thou art not worse to me, and therefore not at all; be careless.

WELFORD
For all things else I would, but for mine honor; Me thinks.

ELDER LOVELESS
Alas, thine honour is not stain'd,
Is this the business that you sent for me about?

MARTHA
Faith Sister you are much to blame, to use a woman, whatsoe're she be, thus; I'le salute her: You are welcome hither.

WELFORD
I humbly thank you.

ELDER LOVELESS
Milde yet as the Dove, for all these injuries. Come shall we goe, I love thee not so ill to keep thee here a jesting stock. Adue to the worlds end.

LADY
Why whither now?

ELDER LOVELESS
Nay you shall never know, because you shall not find me.

LADY
I pray let me speak with you.

ELDER LOVELESS
'Tis very well: come.

LADY
I pray you let me speak with you.

ELDER LOVELESS

Yes for another mock.

LADY
By Heaven I have no mocks: good Sir a word.

ELDER LOVELESS
Though you deserve not so much at my hands, yet if you be in such earnest, I'le speak a word with you; but I beseech you be brief: for in good faith there's a Parson and a licence stay for us i'th' Church all this while: and you know 'tis night.

LADY
Sir, give me hearing patiently, and whatsoever I have heretofore spoke jestingly, forget: for as I hope for mercy any where, what I shall utter now is from my heart, and as I mean.

ELDER LOVELESS
Well, well, what do you mean?

LADY
Was not I once your Mistress, and you my Servant?

ELDER LOVELESS
O 'tis about the old matter.

LADY
Nay good Sir stay me out; I would but hear you excuse your self, why you should take this woman, and leave me.

ELDER LOVELESS
Prethee why not, deserves she not as much as you?

LADY
I think not, if you will look
With an indifferency upon us both.

ELDER LOVELESS
Upon your faces, 'tis true: but if judiciously we shall cast our eyes upon your minds, you are a thousand women of her in worth: she cannot swound in jest, nor set her lover tasks, to shew her peevishness, and his affection, nor cross what he saies, though it be Canonical. She's a good plain wench, that will do as I will have her, and bring me lusty Boys to throw the Sledge, and lift at Pigs of Lead: and for a Wife, she's far beyond you: what can you do in a houshold to provide for your issue, but lye i' bed and get 'em? your business is to dress you, and at idle hours to eat; when she can do a thousand profitable things: she can do pretty well in the Pastry, and knows how Pullen should be cram'd, she cuts Cambrick at a thread, weaves Bone-lace, and quilts Balls; and what are you good for?

LADY
Admit it true, that she were far beyond me in all respects, does that give you a licence to forswear your self?

ELDER LOVELESS
Forswear my self, how?

LADY
Perhaps you have forgotten the innumerable oaths you have utter'd in disclaiming all for Wives but me: I'le not remember you: God give you joy.

ELDER LOVELESS
Nay but conceive me, the intent of oaths is ever understood: Admit I should protest to such a friend, to see him at his Lodging to morrow: Divines would never hold me perjur'd if I were struck blind, or he hid him where my diligent search could not find him: so there were no cross act of mine own in't. Can it be imagined I mean to force you to Marriage, and to have you whether you will or no?

LADY
Alas you need not. I make already tender of my self, and then you are forsworn.

ELDER LOVELESS
Some sin I see indeed must necessarily fall upon me, as whosoever deals with Women shall never utterly avoid it: yet I would chuse the least ill; which is to forsake you, that have done me all the abuses of a malignant Woman, contemn'd my service, and would have held me prating about Marriage, till I had been past getting of Children: then her that hath forsaken her Family, and put her tender body in my hand, upon my word—

LADY
Which of us swore you first to?

ELDER LOVELESS
Why to you.

LADY
Which oath is to be kept then?

ELDER LOVELESS
I prethee do not urge my sins unto me,
Without I could amend 'em.

LADY
Why you may by wedding me.

ELDER LOVELESS
How will that satisfie my word to her?

LADY
'Tis not to be kept, and needs no satisfaction,
'Tis an error fit for repentance only.

ELDER LOVELESS
Shall I live to wrong that tender hearted Virgin so? It may not be.

LADY
Why may it not be?

ELDER LOVELESS
I swear I would rather marry thee than her: but yet mine honesty?

LADY
What honesty? 'Tis more preserv'd this way:
Come, by this light, servant, thou shalt, I'le kiss thee on't.

ELDER LOVELESS
This kiss indeed is sweet, pray God no sin lie under it.

LADY
There is no sin at all, try but another.

WELFORD
O my heart!

MARTHA
Help Sister, this Lady swounds.

ELDER LOVELESS
How do you?

WELFORD
Why very well, if you be so.

ELDER LOVELESS
Since a quiet mind lives not in any Woman, I shall do a most ungodly thing. Hear me one word more, which by all my hopes I will not alter, I did make an oath when you delai'd me so, that this very night I would be married. Now if you will go without delay, suddenly, as late as it is, with your own Minister to your own Chapel, I'le wed you and to bed.

LADY
A match dear servant.

ELDER LOVELESS
For if you should forsake me now, I care not, she would not though for all her injuries, such is her spirit. If I be not ashamed to kiss her now I part, may I not live.

WELFORD
I see you go, as slily as you think to steal away: yet I will pray for you; all blessings of the world light on you two, that you may live to be an aged pair. All curses on me if I do not speak what I do wish indeed.

ELDER LOVELESS
If I can speak to purpose to her, I am a villain.

LADY
Servant away.

MARTHA
Sister, will you Marry that inconstant man? think you he will not cast you off to morrow, to wrong a Lady thus, lookt she like dirt, 'twas basely done. May you ne're prosper with him.

WELFORD
Now God forbid. Alas I was unworthy, so I told him.

MARTHA
That was your modesty, too good for him.
I would not see your wedding for a world.

LADY
Chuse chuse, come Younglove.

[Exit **LADY**, **ELDER LOVELESS**.

MARTHA
Dry up your eyes forsooth, you shall not think we are all such uncivil beasts as these. Would I knew how to give you a revenge.

WELFORD
So would not I: No let me suffer truly, that I desire.

MARTHA
Pray walk in with me, 'tis very late, and you shall stay all night: your bed shall be no worse than mine; I wish I could but do you right.

WELFORD
My humble thanks:
God grant I may but live to quit your love.

[Exeunt.

[Enter **YOUNG LOVELESS** and **SAVIL**.

YOUNG LOVELESS
Did your Master send for me Savil?

SAVIL
Yes, he did send for your worship Sir.

YOUNG LOVELESS
Do you know the business?

SAVIL

Alas Sir, I know nothing, nor am imployed beyond my hours of eating. My dancing days are done Sir.

YOUNG LOVELESS

What art thou now then?

SAVIL

If you consider me in little, I am with your worships reverence Sir, a Rascal: one that upon the next anger of your Brother, must raise a sconce by the high way, and sell switches; my wife is learning now Sir, to weave inkle.

YOUNG LOVELESS

What dost thou mean to do with thy Children Savil?

SAVIL

My eldest boy is half a Rogue already, he was born bursten, and your worship knows, that is a pretty step to mens compassions. My youngest boy I purpose Sir to bind for ten years to a Gaoler, to draw under him, that he may shew us mercy in his function.

YOUNG LOVELESS

Your family is quartered with discretion: you are resolved to
Cant then: where Savil shall your scene lie?

SAVIL

Beggers must be no chusers.
In every place (I take it) but the stocks.

YOUNG LOVELESS

This is your drinking, and your whoring Savil, I told you of it, but your heart was hardened.

SAVIL

'Tis true, you were the first that told me of it I do remember yet in tears, you told me you would have Whores, and in that passion Sir, you broke out thus; Thou miserable man, repent, and brew three Strikes more in a Hogshead. 'Tis noon e're we be drunk now, and the time can tarry for no man.

YOUNG LOVELESS

Y'are grown a bitter Gentleman. I see misery can clear your head better than Mustard, I'le be a sutor for your Keys again Sir.

SAVIL

Will you but be so gracious to me Sir? I shall be bound.

YOUNG LOVELESS

You shall Sir
To your bunch again, or I'le miss foully.

[Enter **MORECRAFT**.

MORECRAFT
Save you Gentleman, save you.

YOUNG LOVELESS
Now Polecat, what young Rabets nest have you to draw?

MORECRAFT
Come, prethee be familiar Knight.

YOUNG LOVELESS
Away Fox, I'le send for Terriers for you.

MORECRAFT
Thou art wide yet: I'le keep thee companie.

YOUNG LOVELESS
I am about some business; Indentures,
If ye follow me I'le beat you: take heed,
As I live I'le cancel your Coxcomb.

MORECRAFT
Thou art cozen'd now, I am no usurer:
What poor fellow's this?

SAVIL
I am poor indeed Sir.

MORECRAFT
Give him mony Knight.

YOUNG LOVELESS
Do you begin the offering.

MORECRAFT
There poor fellow, here's an Angel for thee.

YOUNG LOVELESS
Art thou in earnest Morecraft?

MORECRAFT
Yes faith Knight, I'le follow thy example: thou hadst land and thousands, thou spendst, and flungst away, and yet it flows in double: I purchased, wrung, and wierdraw'd, for my wealth, lost, and was cozen'd: for which I make a vow, to trie all the waies above ground, but I'le find a constant means to riches without curses.

YOUNG LOVELESS
I am glad of your conversion Master Morecraft:
Y'are in a fair course, pray pursue it still.

MORECRAFT

Come, we are all gallants now, I'le keep thee company; Here honest fellow, for this Gentlemans sake, there's two Angels more for thee.

SAVIL

God quite you Sir, and keep you long in this mind.

YOUNG LOVELESS

Wilt thou persevere?

MORECRAFT

Till I have a penny. I have brave cloathes a making, and two horses; canst thou not help me to a match Knight, I'le lay a thousand pound upon my crop-ear.

YOUNG LOVELESS

Foot, this is stranger than an Africk monster,
There will be no more talk of the Cleve wars
Whilst this lasts, come, I'le put thee into blood.

SAVIL

Would all his damn'd tribe were as tender hearted. I beseech you let this Gentleman join with you in the recovery of my Keyes; I like his good beginning Sir, the whilst I'le pray for both your worships.

YOUNG LOVELESS

He shall Sir.

MORECRAFT

Shall we goe noble Knight? I would fain be acquainted.

YOUNG LOVELESS

I'le be your Servant Sir.

[Exeunt.

[Enter **ELDER LOVELESS**, and **LADY**.

ELDER LOVELESS

Faith my sweet Lady, I have caught you now, maugre your subtilties, and fine devices, be coy again now.

LADY

Prethee sweet-heart tell true.

ELDER LOVELESS

By this light, by all the pleasures I have had this night, by your lost maidenhead, you are cozened meerly. I have cast beyond your wit. That Gentleman is your retainer Welford.

LADY

It cannot be so.

ELDER LOVELESS
Your Sister has found it so, or I mistake, mark how she blushes when you see her next. Ha, ha, ha, I shall not travel now, ha, ha, ha.

LADY
Prethee sweet heart be quiet, thou hast angred me at heart.

ELDER LOVELESS
I'le please you soon again.

LADY
Welford?

ELDER LOVELESS
I Welford, hee's a young handsome fellow, well bred and landed, your Sister can instruct you in his good parts, better than I by this time.

LADY
Uds foot am I fetcht over thus?

ELDER LOVELESS
Yes i'faith.
And over shall be fetcht again, never fear it.

LADY
I must be patient, though it torture me:
You have got the Sun Sir.

ELDER LOVELESS
And the Moon too, in which I'le be the man.

LADY
But had I known this, had I but surmiz'd it, you should have hunted three trains more, before you had come to th' course, you should have hankt o'th' bridle, Sir, i'faith.

ELDER LOVELESS
I knew it, and min'd with you, and so blew you up.
Now you may see the Gentlewoman: stand close.

[Enter **WELFORD** and **MARTHA**.

MARTHA
For Gods sake Sir, be private in this business,
You have undone me else. O God, what have I done?

WELFORD

No harm I warrant thee.

MARTHA
How shall I look upon my friends again?
With what face?

WELFORD
Why e'ne with that: 'tis a good one, thou canst not find a better: look upon all the faces thou shall see there, and you shall find 'em smooth still, fair still, sweet still, and to your thinking honest; those have done as much as you have yet, or dare doe Mistris, and yet they keep no stir.

MARTHA
Good Sir goe in, and put your womans cloaths on:
If you be seen thus, I am lost for ever.

WELFORD
I'le watch you for that Mistris: I am no fool, here will I tarry till the house be up and witness with me.

MARTHA
Good dear friend goe in.

WELFORD
To bed again if you please, else I am fixt here till there be notice taken what I am, and what I have done: if you could juggle me into my woman-hood again, and so cog me out of your company, all this would be forsworn, and I again an asinego, as your Sister left me. No, I'le have it known and publisht; then if you'le be a whore, forsake me and be asham'd: and when you can hold no longer, marry some cast Cleve Captain, and sell Bottle-ale.

MARTHA
I dare not stay Sir, use me modestly, I am your wife.

WELFORD
Goe in, I'le make up all.

ELDER LOVELESS
I'le be a witness of your naked truth Sir: this is the Gentlewoman, prethee look upon him, that is he that made me break my faith sweet: but thank your Sister, she hath soder'd it.

LADY
What a dull ass was I, I could not see this wencher from a wench: twenty to one, if I had been but tender like my Sister, he had served me such a slippery trick too.

WELFORD
Twenty to one I had.

ELDER LOVELESS
I would have watcht you Sir, by your good patience, for ferreting in my ground.

LADY
You have been with my Sister.

WELFORD
Yes to bring.

ELDER LOVELESS
An heir into the world he means.

LADY
There is no chafing now.

WELFORD
I have had my part on't: I have been chaft this three hours, that's the least, I am reasonable cool now.

LADY
Cannot you fare well, but you must cry roast-meat?

WELFORD
He that fares well, and will not bless the founders, is either surfeited, or ill taught, Lady, for mine own part, I have found so sweet a diet, I can commend it, though I cannot spare it.

ELDER LOVELESS
How like you this dish, Welford, I made a supper on't, and fed so heartily, I could not sleep.

LADY
By this light, had I but scented out your train, ye had slept with a bare pillow in your arms and kist that, or else the bed-post, for any wife ye had got this twelve-month yet: I would have vext you more than a try'd post-horse; and been longer bearing, than ever after-game at Irish was. Lord, that I were unmarried again.

ELDER LOVELESS
Lady I would not undertake ye, were you again a Haggard, for the best cast of four Ladys i'th' Kingdom: you were ever tickle-footed, and would not truss round.

WELFORD
Is she fast?

ELDER LOVELESS
She was all night lockt here boy.

WELFORD
Then you may lure her without fear of losing: take off her Cranes. You have a delicate Gentlewoman to your Sister: Lord what a prettie furie she was in, when she perceived I was a man: but I thank God I satisfied her scruple, without the Parson o'th' town.

ELDER LOVELESS
What did ye?

WELFORD
Madam, can you tell what we did?

ELDER LOVELESS
She has a shrewd guess at it I see it by her.

LADY
Well you may mock us: but my large Gentlewoman, my Mary Ambre, had I but seen into you, you should
have had another bed-fellow, fitter a great deal for your itch.

WELFORD
I thank you Lady, me thought it was well,
You are so curious.

[Enter **YOUNG LOVELESS**, his **LADY**, **MORECRAFT**, **SAVIL** and two **SERVING MEN**.

ELDER LOVELESS
Get on your doublet, here comes my Brother.

YOUNG LOVELESS
Good morrow Brother, and all good to your Lady.

MORECRAFT
God save you and good morrow to you all.

ELDER LOVELESS
Good morrow. Here's a poor brother of yours.

LADY
Fie how this shames me.

MORECRAFT
Prethee good fellow help me to a cup of beer.

SERVANT
I will Sir.

YOUNG LOVELESS
Brother what makes you here? will this Lady do?
Will she? is she not nettl'd still?

ELDER LOVELESS
No I have cur'd her.
Mr. Welford, pray know this Gentleman is my Brother.

WELFORD
Sir I shall long to love him.

YOUNG LOVELESS
I shall not be your debter Sir. But how is't with you?

ELDER LOVELESS
As well as may be man: I am married: your new acquaintance hath her Sister, and all's well.

YOUNG LOVELESS
I am glad on't. Now my prettie Lady Sister,
How do you find my Brother?

LADY
Almost as wild as you are.

YOUNG LOVELESS
He will make the better husband: you have tried him?

LADY
Against my will Sir.

YOUNG LOVELESS
Hee'l make your will amends soon, do not doubt it.
But Sir I must intreat you to be better known
To this converted Jew here.

SERVANT
Here's Beer for you Sir.

MORECRAFT
And here's for you an Angel:
Pray buy no Land, 'twill never prosper Sir.

ELDER LOVELESS
How's this?

YOUNG LOVELESS
Bless you, and then I'le tell: He's turn'd Gallant.

ELDER LOVELESS
Gallant?

YOUNG LOVELESS
I Gallant, and is now called, Cutting Morecraft:
The reason I'le inform you at more leisure.

WELFORD
O good Sir let me know him presently.

YOUNG LOVELESS
You shall hug one another.

MORECRAFT
Sir I must keep you company.

ELDER LOVELESS
And reason.

YOUNG LOVELESS
Cutting Morecraft faces about, I must present another.

MORECRAFT
As many as you will Sir, I am for 'em.

WELFORD
Sir I shall do you service.

MORECRAFT
I shall look for't in good faith Sir.

ELDER LOVELESS
Prethee good sweet heart kiss him.

LADY
Who, that fellow?

SAVIL
Sir will it please you to remember me: my keys good Sir.

YOUNG LOVELESS
I'le doe it presently.

ELDER LOVELESS
Come thou shalt kiss him for our sport sake.

LADY
Let him come on then; and do you hear, do not instruct me in these tricks, for you may repent it.

ELDER LOVELESS
That at my peril. Lusty Mr. Morecraft,
Here is a Lady would salute you.

MORECRAFT
She shall not lose her longing Sir: what is she?

ELDER LOVELESS
My wife Sir.

MORECRAFT
She must be then my Mistres.

LADY
Must I Sir?

ELDER LOVELESS
O yes, you must.

MORECRAFT
And you must take this ring, a poor pawn
Of some fiftie pound.

ELDER LOVELESS
Take it by any means, 'tis lawfull prize.

LADY
Sir I shall call you servant.

MORECRAFT
I shall be proud on't: what fellow's that?

YOUNG LOVELESS
My Ladies Coachman.

MORECRAFT
There's something, (my friend) for you to buy whips,
And for you Sir, and you Sir.

ELDER LOVELESS
Under a miracle this is the strangest
I ever heard of.

MORECRAFT
What, shall we play, or drink? what shall we doe?
Who will hunt with me for a hundred pounds?

WELFORD
Stranger and Stranger!
Sir you shall find sport after a day or two.

YOUNG LOVELESS
Sir I have a sute unto you
Concerning your old servant Savil.

ELDER LOVELESS
O, for his keys, I know it.

SAVIL
Now Sir, strike in.

MORECRAFT
Sir I must have you grant me.

ELDER LOVELESS
'Tis done Sir, take your keys again:
But hark you Savil, leave off the motions
Of the flesh, and be honest, or else you shall graze again:
I'le try you once more.

SAVIL
If ever I be taken drunk, or whoring,
Take off the biggest key i'th' bunch, and open
My head with it Sir: I humbly thank your worships.

ELDER LOVELESS
Nay then I see we must keep holiday.
Enter Roger, and Abigal.
Here's the last couple in hell.

SIR ROGER
Joy be among you all.

LADY
Why how now Sir, what is the meaning of this emblem?

SIR ROGER
Marriage an't like your worship.

LADY
Are you married?

SIR ROGER
As well as the next Priest could doe it, Madam.

ELDER LOVELESS
I think the sign's in Gemini, here's such coupling.

WELFORD
Sir Roger, what will you take to lie from your sweet-heart to night?

SIR ROGER
Not the best benefice in your worships gift Sir.

WELFORD

A whorson, how he swells.

YOUNG LOVELESS
How many times to night Sir Roger?

SIR ROGER
Sir you grow scurrilous:
What I shall do, I shall do: I shall not need your help.

YOUNG LOVELESS
For horse flesh Roger.

ELDER LOVELESS
Come prethee be not angry, 'tis a day
Given wholly to our mirth.

LADY
It shall be so Sir: Sir Roger and his Bride,
We shall intreat to be at our charge.

ELDER LOVELESS
Welford get you to the Church: by this light,
You shall not lie with her again, till y'are married.

WELFORD
I am gone.

MORECRAFT
To every Bride I dedicate this day
Six healths a piece, and it shall goe hard,
But every one a Jewell: Come be mad boys.

ELDER LOVELESS
Th'art in a good beginning: come who leads?
Sir Roger, you shall have the Van: lead the way:
Would every dogged wench had such a day.

[Exeunt.

Francis Beaumont – A Short Biography

Francis Beaumont was born in 1584 near the small Leicestershire village of Thringstone. Unfortunately precise records of much of his short life do not exist.

He was the son to Sir Francis Beaumont of Grace Dieu, a justice of the common pleas. His mother was Anne, the daughter of Sir George Pierrepont.

The first date we can give for his education is at age 13 when he begins at Broadgates Hall (now Pembroke College, Oxford). Sadly, his father died the following year, 1598. Beaumont left university without a degree and entered the Inner Temple in London in 1600. A career choice of Law taken previously by his father.

The information to hand is confident that Beaumont's career in law was short-lived. He was quickly attracted to the theatre and soon became first an admirer and then a student of poet and playwright Ben Jonson. Jonson at this time was a cultural behemoth; very talented and a life full of volatility that included frequent brushes with the authorities. His followers, including the poet Robert Herrick, were known as 'the sons of Ben'. Beaumont was also on friendly terms with other luminaries such as the poet Michael Drayton.

Beaumont's first work was Salmacis and Hermaphroditus, it debuted in 1602. A 1911 edition of the Encyclopædia Britannica includes the description "not on the whole discreditable to a lad of eighteen, fresh from the popular love-poems of Marlowe and Shakespeare, which it naturally exceeds in long-winded and fantastic diffusion of episodes and conceits."

By 1605, Beaumont had written commendatory verses to Volpone one of Ben Jonson's masterpieces.

It was now, in the early years of the 17th Century, that he met John Fletcher and together they gradually formed one of the most dynamic and productive of writing teams that English theatre has ever produced.

Their playwriting careers at this stage were both troubled by early failure. Beaumont had written The Knight of the Burning Pestle and it was first performed by the Children of the Blackfriars company in 1607. The audience however was distinctly unimpressed. The publisher's epistle in the 1613 quarto says they failed to note "the privie mark of irony about it."

The following year, Fletcher's Faithful Shepherdess failed on the same stage.

In 1609, however, the two collaborated in earnest on Philaster. The play was performed by the King's Men at the Globe Theatre and at Blackfriars. It was a great success. Their careers were now well and truly launched and into the bargain they had ignited and captured a public taste for tragicomedy.

There is an account that at the time the two men shared everything. They lived together in a house on the Bankside in Southwark, " they also lived together in Bankside, sharing clothes and having "one wench in the house between them." Or as another account puts it "sharing everything in the closest intimacy."

This arrangement stopped in about 1613 when Beaumont married Ursula Isley, daughter and co-heiress of Henry Isley of Sundridge in Kent, by whom he had two daughters (one of them was born after his death).

Beaumont, at a very young age even for those times, was struck down by a stroke at some point in mid-1613, after which he was unable to write any more plays, but he did manage to write an elegy for Lady Penelope Clifton, who had died on 26th October 1613.

Francis Beaumont died on March 6th, 1616 and was buried in Westminster Abbey.

In his short life his canon was small but influential. Although he is seen more as a dramatist his poetry was celebrated even then and it continues to gain an avid readership to this day.

It was said at one point of the collaboration of Beaumont and Fletcher that "in their joint plays their talents are so ... completely merged into one, that the hand of Beaumont cannot clearly be distinguished from that of Fletcher." Whilst it was the view then it has not endured into modern times. Indeed, slowly but with certainty the name of Beaumont has been removed from many of their joint works. It has given way to other such luminaries as Philip Massinger, Nathan field and James Shirley.

John Fletcher – A Short Biography

John Fletcher was born in December, 1579 in Rye, Sussex. He was baptised on December 20th.

As can be imagined details of much of his life and career have not survived and, accordingly, only a very brief indication of his life and works can be given.

His father, Richard Fletcher, was a successful and rather ambitious cleric. From being the Dean of Peterborough he moved on to become the Bishop of Bristol, Bishop of Worcester and finally, shortly before his death, the Bishop of London. He was also the chaplain to Queen Elizabeth.

When he was Dean of Peterborough, Richard Fletcher, witnessed the execution of Mary, Queen of Scots. It was said he "knelt down on the scaffold steps and started to pray out loud and at length, in a prolonged and rhetorical style, as though determined to force his way into the pages of history". He cried out at her death, "So perish all the Queen's enemies!" All very dramatic but the family did have strong links to the Arts.

Young Fletcher appears at the very young age of eleven to have entered Corpus Christi College at Cambridge University in 1591. There are no records that he ever took a degree but there is some small evidence that he was being prepared for a career in the church.

However, what is clear is that this was soon abandoned as he joined the stream of people who would leave University and decamp to the more bohemian life of commercial theatre in London.

Unfortunately, his father fell out with Queen Elizabeth but appears to have been on his way to rehabilitation before his death in 1596. At his death he was, however, mired in debt.

The upbringing of the now teenage Fletcher and his seven siblings now passed to his paternal uncle, the poet and minor official Giles Fletcher. Giles, who had the patronage of the Earl of Essex may have been a liability rather than an advantage to the young Fletcher. With Essex involved in the failed rebellion against Elizabeth Giles was also tainted by association.

By 1606 John Fletcher appears to have equipped himself with the talents to become a playwright. Initially this appears to have been for the Children of the Queen's Revels, then performing at the Blackfriars Theatre.

Commendatory verses by Richard Brome in the Beaumont and Fletcher 1647 folio place Fletcher in the company of Ben Jonson, although it is not known when this friendship began. Jonson, of course, was a leviathan of English Literature, so admired that many of his literary friends and colleagues were simply known as 'Sons of Ben'. Fletcher's frequent early collaborator, Francis Beaumont, was also a friend of Jonson's.

Fletcher's early career was marked by one significant failure; The Faithful Shepherdess, his adaptation of Giovanni Battista Guarini's Il Pastor Fido, which was performed by the Blackfriars Children in 1608. In the preface to the printed edition of his play, Fletcher explained the failure as due to his audience's faulty expectations. They expected a pastoral tragicomedy to feature dances, comedy, and murder, with the shepherds presented in conventional stereotypes – as Fletcher put it, wearing "gray cloaks, with curtailed dogs in strings." Fletcher's preface is however best known for its pithy definition of tragicomedy: "A tragicomedy is not so called in respect of mirth and killing, but in respect it wants [i.e., lacks] deaths, which is enough to make it no tragedy; yet brings some near it, which is enough to make it no comedy." A comedy, he went on to say, must be "a representation of familiar people." His preface is critical of drama that features characters whose action violates nature.

In that case, Fletcher appears to have been developing a new style faster than audiences could comprehend. By 1609, however, he had found his stride. With Beaumont, he wrote Philaster, which became a hit for the King's Men and began a profitable association between Fletcher and that company. Philaster appears also to have begun a trend for tragicomedy. Fletcher's influence has also been said to have inspired some features of Shakespeare's late romances, and certainly his influence on the tragicomic work of other playwrights is even more marked.

By the middle of the 1610s, Fletcher's plays had achieved a popularity that rivalled Shakespeare's and cemented the pre-eminence of the King's Men in Jacobean London. After Beaumont's retirement, necessitated by ill-health, and then his early death in 1616, Fletcher continued working, both singly and in collaboration, until his death in 1625. By that time, he had produced, or had been credited with, close to fifty plays. This body of work remained a major part of the King's Men's repertory until the closing of the theatres in 1642 due to the Civil War.

At the beginning of his career Fletcher's most important collaborator was Francis Beaumont. The two wrote together for close to a decade, first for the Children of the Queen's Revels, and then for the King's Men. According to an anecdote transmitted or invented by John Aubrey, they also lived together in Bankside, sharing clothes and having "one wench in the house between them." This domestic arrangement, if it existed, was ended by Beaumont's marriage in 1613, and their dramatic partnership ended after Beaumont fell ill, probably of a stroke, that same year.

At this point Fletcher had written many plays with Beaumont and several others on his own. He seems to have been regarded as quite a talent although it should be remembered that playwrights were required to be prolific, to easily work with other collaborators and to produce work of quality and commercial appeal very quickly.

The King's Men, run by Philip Henslowe, was the most prestigious of the theatre companies and Fletcher now had an increasingly close association with it.

Fletcher collaborated with Shakespeare on Henry VIII, The Two Noble Kinsmen, and the now lost Cardenio, which some scholars say was the basis for Lewis Theobald's play Double Falsehood. (Theobald is regarded as one of the best Shakespearean editors. Whether his play is based on Cardenio or on some other is not absolutely known although Theobald certainly promoted it as his revision of the lost Shakespeare/Fletcher play.)

A play that Fletcher also wrote by himself at this time, The Woman's Prize or the Tamer Tamed, is also regarded as a sequel to The Taming of the Shrew.

In 1616, with the death of Shakespeare, Fletcher now appears to have entered into an enhanced arrangement with the King's Men on very similar terms to Shakespeare's. Fletcher would now write exclusively for the King's Men until his own death almost a decade later.

As well as continuing his solo productions Fletcher was still collaborating with other playwrights, mainly Philip Massinger, who, in turn, would succeed him as the in-house playwright for the King's Men.

Fletcher's popularity continued throughout his life; indeed, during the winter of 1621, he had three of his plays performed at court. His mastery is most notable in two dramatic types; tragicomedy and the comedy of manners.

John Fletcher died in 1625, it is thought of bubonic plague which, at the time, was undergoing further outbreaks.

He seems to have been buried in what is now Southwark Cathedral, although a precise location is not known. There is much made of an anecdote that Fletcher and Massinger (who died in 1640) share the same grave but it is more likely that both are buried within a few yards of each other and that the stone markers in the floor have confused the issue. One is marked 'Edmond Shakespeare 1607' and the other 'John Fletcher 1625' refers to Shakespeare's younger brother and the playwright. The churchyards were, more often than not, completely over-crowded and breeding grounds for disease. Precise record keeping was not a practiced skill.

During the later Commonwealth, many of the playwright's best-known scenes were kept alive as drolls. These were brief performances, usually condensed into one or two scenes and with the addition of music or song to satisfy the taste for plays while the theatres were closed under the Puritans. At the re-opening of the theatres in 1660, the plays in the Fletcher canon, in original form or revised, were by far the most common productions on the English stage. The most frequently revived plays suggest the developing taste for comedies of manners. Among the tragedies, The Maid's Tragedy and, especially, Rollo Duke of Normandy held the stage. Four tragicomedies (A King and No King, The Humorous Lieutenant, Philaster, and The Island Princess) were popular, perhaps in part for their similarity to and foreshadowing of heroic drama. Four comedies (Rule a Wife And Have a Wife, The Chances, Beggars' Bush, and especially The Scornful Lady) were also stage mainstays.

Despite his popularity, and it appears he was held in higher regard than Shakespeare at this time, his works steadily lost ground to those of Shakespeare and to new productions from other playwrights.

Since then Fletcher has increasingly become a subject only for occasional revivals and for specialists. Fletcher and his collaborators have been the subject of important bibliographic and critical studies, but the plays have been revived only infrequently.

Due to the frequent collaborations between all manner of playwrights, and the revisions carried out in later years, having a settled list of authorship to any given set of plays can be problematic. The works of Fletcher and others of this period most definitely fall into this category. It is as well to take into account that during this period theatres were quite often closed either due to outbreaks of the plague or to the prevailing political and moral climate. Printers, anxious to provide materials that would sell, were not above changing a name or two to enhance sales.

Although Fletcher collaborated most often with Beaumont and Massinger, it is believed that Massinger revised many of the plays some time after their original production. Other collaborators including Nathan Field, William Shakespeare, William Rowley and others also can be seen distinctly in Fletchers' works. Many modern scholars point out that Fletcher had many particular mannerisms, but other playwrights would also duplicate these at times so allocating exact contributions of anyone to a play is somewhat of a detective case in many instances. However, from the original folio printings or licensing via the Master of the Revels (the statutory licensing authority to approve and censor plays as well a hand in publication and printing of theatrical materials) as well as contemporary notes a fairly precise bibliography of the works can be given with only a few plays lacking substantial authority and provenance.

Francis Beaumont & John Fletcher – A Concise Bibliography

This bibliography gives the most likely date of writing together with when published, revised or licensed by the Master or the Revels (This position within the royal household was originally for royal festivities, ie revels, and later to oversee stage censorship, until this function was transferred to the Lord Chamberlain in 1624).

Francis Beaumont – Solo Plays
The Knight of the Burning Pestle, comedy (performed 1607; printed 1613)
The Masque of the Inner Temple and Gray's Inn, masque (printed 1613)

John Fletcher - Solo Plays
The Faithful Shepherdess, pastoral (written 1608–9; printed 1609)
The Tragedy of Valentinian, tragedy (1610–14; 1647)
Monsieur Thomas, comedy (c. 1610–16; 1639)
The Woman's Prize, or The Tamer Tamed, comedy (c. 1611; 1647)
Bonduca, tragedy (1611–14; 1647)
The Chances, comedy (c. 1613–25; 1647)
Wit Without Money, comedy (c. 1614; 1639)
The Mad Lover, tragicomedy (acted 5 January 1617; 1647)
The Loyal Subject, tragicomedy (licensed 16 November 1618; revised 1633; 1647)
The Humorous Lieutenant, tragicomedy (c. 1619; 1647)
Women Pleased, tragicomedy (c. 1619–23; 1647)
The Island Princess, tragicomedy (c. 1620; 1647)
The Wild Goose Chase, comedy (c. 1621; 1652)
The Pilgrim, comedy (c. 1621; 1647)
A Wife for a Month, tragicomedy (licensed 27 May 1624; 1647)

Rule a Wife and Have a Wife, comedy (licensed 19 October 1624; 1640)

Francis Beaumont & John Fletcher
The Woman Hater, comedy (1606; 1607)
Cupid's Revenge, tragedy (c. 1607–12; 1615)
Philaster, or Love Lies a-Bleeding, tragicomedy (c. 1609; 1620)
The Maid's Tragedy, Tragedy (c. 1609; 1619)
A King and No King, tragicomedy (1611; 1619)
The Captain, comedy (c. 1609–12; 1647)
The Scornful Lady, comedy (c. 1613; 1616)
Love's Pilgrimage, tragicomedy (c. 1615–16; 1647)
The Noble Gentleman, comedy (c. 1613; licensed 3 February 1626; 1647)

Their Collaborations with Others

With Philip Massinger
Thierry & Theodoret, tragedy (c. 1607; 1621)
The Coxcomb, comedy (c. 1608–10; 1647)
Beggars' Bush, comedy (c. 1612–13; revised 1622; 1647)
Love's Cure, comedy (c. 1612–13; revised 1625; 1647)

John Fletcher with Philip Massinger
Sir John van Olden Barnavelt, tragedy (August 1619; MS)
The Little French Lawyer, comedy (c. 1619–23; 1647)
A Very Woman, tragicomedy (c. 1619–22; licensed 6 June 1634; 1655)
The Custom of the Country, comedy (c. 1619–23; 1647)
The Double Marriage, tragedy (c. 1619–23; 1647)
The False One, history (c. 1619–23; 1647)
The Prophetess, tragicomedy (licensed 14 May 1622; 1647)
The Sea Voyage, comedy (licensed 22 June 1622; 1647)
The Spanish Curate, comedy (licensed 24 October 1622; 1647)
The Lovers' Progress or The Wandering Lovers, tragicomedy (licensed 6 December 1623; rev 1634; 1647)
The Elder Brother, comedy (c. 1625; 1637)

John Fletcher with Philip Massinger & Nathan Field
The Honest Man's Fortune, tragicomedy (1613; 1647)
The Queen of Corinth, tragicomedy (c. 1616–18; 1647)
The Knight of Malta, tragicomedy (c. 1619; 1647)

John Fletcher with William Shakespeare
Henry VIII, history (c. 1613; 1623)
The Two Noble Kinsmen, tragicomedy (c. 1613; 1634)
Cardenio, tragicomedy (c. 1613)

John Fletcher with Thomas Middleton & William Rowley
Wit at Several Weapons, comedy (c. 1610–20; 1647)

John Fletcher with William Rowley

The Maid in the Mill (licensed 29 August 1623; 1647).

John Fletcher with Nathan Field
Four Plays, or Moral Representations, in One, morality (c. 1608–13; 1647)

John Fletcher with Philip Massinger, Ben Jonson and George Chapman
Rollo Duke of Normandy, or The Bloody Brother, tragedy (c. 1617; revised 1627–30; 1639)

John Fletcher with James Shirley
The Night Walker, or The Little Thief, comedy (c. 1611; 1640)
The Coronation c. 1635

Uncertain
The Nice Valour, or The Passionate Madman, comedy (c. 1615–25; 1647)
The Laws of Candy, tragicomedy (c. 1619–23; 1647)
The Fair Maid of the Inn, comedy (licensed 22 January 1626; 1647)
The Faithful Friends, tragicomedy (registered 29 June 1660; MS.)

The Nice Valour is possibly by Fletcher revised by Thomas Middleton;

The Fair Maid of the Inn is perhaps a play by Massinger, John Ford, and John Webster, either with or without Fletcher's involvement.

The Laws of Candy has been variously attributed to Fletcher and to John Ford.

The Night-Walker was a Fletcher original, with additions by Shirley for a 1639 production.

Even now there is not absolute certainty on several of the plays. The first Beaumont & Fletcher folio of 1647 contained 35 plays and the second folio of 1679 added a further 18. In total 53 plays.

The first folio included The Masque of the Inner Temple and Gray's Inn (1613), and the second The Knight of the Burning Pestle (1607), widely considered Beaumont's solo works, although the latter was in early editions attributed to both writers. Fletcher himself said that Beaumont was attributed co-authorship of many works that belonged solely to Fletcher or to other collaborators.

One play in the canon, Sir John Van Olden Barnavelt, existed in manuscript and was not published till 1883.